AF424482

EXTERMINATE OR EVOLVE

Octogenarians Opine about the Violent Gun Culture in America

JAMES KILGORE

Copyright © 2026 by James Kilgore.

All rights reserved. No part of this publication may be reproduced, distributed, or transmitted in any form or by any electronic or mechanical means, including information storage and retrieval systems, without a prior written permission from the publisher, except by reviewers, who may quote brief passages in a review, and certain other noncommercial uses permitted by the copyright law.

ISBN: 979-8-90252-156-3   (Paperback)
ISBN: 979-8-90252-157-0   (eBook)

Printed in the United States of America

CONTENTS

With much gratitude...

You wouldn't be holding this book in your hands if it weren't for a very special helper, my daughter, Laura Kilgore Ise, who was my primary editor and the one who helped me with my vision disabilities. I also wish to thank all those who work to lobby for gun control and regulations in organizations such as Everytown for Gun Safety, Brady United Against Gun Violence, and the Giffords Law Center to Prevent Gun Violence, as well as the politicians and supporters of these organizations who are doing something to reduce gun violence in our country. I also appreciate all those who have conducted extensive research and written articles and books on the subject. Finally, I wish to acknowledge Wendy Herbert, a friend who helped me get the manuscript to the publisher.

CHAPTER ONE

Roberto finished reading his newspaper, sitting in his easy chair in his living room. He checked his smartphone for any texts before he went into his office to check the stock market and new emails on his computer. Then it was time for the Tuesday and Thursday Zoom chat at 3:00 p.m. MDT. He clicked on the Zoom link for the *Octogenarians Opine* chat room.

Rx: That's what you should do. You need the sleep.

PM: I take Tylenol almost every night to relieve the aches from my right hip.

KO: Hi, aches-and-pains people. You sound like a bunch of old fogies.

YY: Yeah, I think I'll talk with my doc about the pain meds. I'm feeling sleep-deprived

KO: Speaking of aches and pains, did any of you hear about the two kids in Florida, who broke into a house and found some guns and wound up having a shootout with the police?

Rx: I wonder if See Saw will join us today. He was supposed to have an MRI exam this morning for his lower back problem.

PM: Yes, Roberto, the incident was reported on one of the news shows on TV. Apparently, two kids, twelve and fourteen, left a children's home at a Methodist church, broke into an unoccupied home. Neighbors called the police when they heard glass breaking. The homeowner told the police he had an AK-47, a pump-action shotgun, and a handgun. The police were ready for action in Volusia County, Florida.

YY: I hope Shahzad doesn't have to go through the suffering I went through. I had an MRI and then surgery for my torn muscle tissue. It took months of PT and aching before I felt better. Thanks for the police report, Mark.

KO: Can you imagine having a shootout with the police when you were twelve or even fourteen? The fourteen-year-old girl got shot, but she's going to live.

Rx: PM and KO, you shouldn't be so surprised at what happened with those kids. Kids are killing each other almost daily in big cities.

PM: Rx, I mean, Clyde, I think I see something that looks like a gun cabinet in the far-left corner of the room you're in.

YY: What's a little nerve-racking is that those kids found a semiautomatic rifle in that house, and the girl was using it on the cops!

Rx: Hey, Mark, I thought you weren't a patrolman any longer. You sure are kind of snoopy. That is a gun cabinet. I've had those long guns a long time and haven't killed anyone with them yet.

PM: Yes, Rx, my eyes are trained to spot guns. I'm no longer a patrolman; I rose in the ranks to commander, you know. What kind of long guns do you have? Any semiautos? I know all too well that kids do a lot of the killing in this country. Sometimes, they use a family gun to kill another family member or friend. That's why guns need to be stored in a vault-like cabinet.

KO: Obviously, the guns those kids found in that house weren't stored in a vault-like cabinet. Mark, about how many kids kill family members or friends using family-owned guns in their own homes every year in the U.S.?

YY: Those kids who kill a family member or a friend don't do that intentionally, right? In my native country, most people don't own or have guns in their homes, and as a result, there's no killing with guns in the home.

PM: Right, Yoshi, most of the deaths are accidental, upwards of a hundred a year, Roberto. The parents are devastated. Most of the time, the gun(s) were out of sight and unfortunately, out of mind, except for the kids.

SW: Hi, everyone. It sounds like you guys are opining on another serious topic.

Rx: See Saw, Mark, Yoshi, and Roberto have already put their stakes down on a new topic: guns and killing with guns. No more opining about immigration.

KO: That's our topic for now. Mark and I think it's a very important one. How did your MRI go, Shahzad? Any results yet?

SW: No, Roberto, no results yet. I'm glad it's over with for now.

YY: Speaking of shootings, I'm sure all of you saw on TV and read in the papers

YY: that massacre in Las Vegas a few years back. One of my partners was in Vegas near where it took place. He actually heard some of the shooting and people screaming and yelling. He was not at the concert. He was... emotionally drained when he called me the next day.

Rx: How could anyone living in this country avoid hearing about that atrocity? The news media went berserk over that event for weeks on end.

PM: Even though you may not wish to recall that event, it happened in October 2017 with the killer shooting from the thirty-second floor of the Mandalay Bay hotel-casino. At least fifty-nine concertgoers were killed, and over five hundred were wounded or injured. The killer had something like twenty-three guns in his room. I was informed of quite a number of mass shootings during my law enforcement career, but that murderous rampage was extraordinarily terrible.

SW: How can anyone buy that many guns without some red flags waving in the ATF federal agency?

PM: There are quite a few gun collectors in this country and they own a lot of guns. That guy named Paddock actually owned around forty guns.

KO: Mark, speaking of kids being killed, that Newtown school shooting was unbelievable. That guy took an AK-47 into that school and took the lives of very young kids in first and second grades and some teachers. We've got to prevent a sick SOB from getting his hands on an AK-47 rifle. Unbelievable!

YY: There's another lunatic with a gun. I thought the federal government did background checks on people buying guns, especially those kinds of guns.

SW: Mark, about what percentage of gun owners are collectors? Do they own a big percentage of the guns owned by private parties in the U.S.?

PM: Yes, Yoshi, there are background checks if someone buys a gun in a gun shop, but lots of people buy guns at gun shows, from family members, and friends, and lots of them are stolen in burglaries. That "lunatic" actually took his mother's gun that morning. Roberto, it was an AR-15, just as bad.

Rx: It sounds like you gentlemen are blaming the guns, not the humans who load the ammunition and pull the triggers.

PM: Shahzad, let me get back to you with some info on your question.

KO: Here's a little more info on the Newtown shooting: According to an article I just looked up, it was the deadliest mass shooting at an elementary school in U.S. history.

YY: Why are Americans letting this happen over and over again?

SW: I watched President Obama talking about this terrible killing of schoolkids on TV, and he began to cry. Before I could control myself, I was crying too. It was very sad!

PM: I've got some errands to run, but to this day, some nonbelievers believe that mass shooting was made up to promote gun control. They don't believe the parents who lost their kids, the teachers, the police or government officials, or the coroners. See you youngsters on Thursday.

Rx: There is a big portion of the media that is always looking for a story to use to promote the reduction of gun ownership rights in this country. You have to admit that if you wish to have credibility with me.

KO: The most outspoken radio commentator, Mark, said he didn't believe all that was reported about the Sandy Hook massacre, He said it was a hoax I've got to join Mark in saying adios for now.

Rx: See what I mean? The media selected Alex Jones to degrade the questioning of reporting of homicides that include guns. There were many gun-rights spokespeople lamenting how terrible it was that that sick young man got hold of his mother's legally possessed firearm to commit that tragedy. I don't wish to put my pharmacist hat on, but some of you need to medicate with truth serum. I'm leaving my pharmacy. Good afternoon.

SW: Yoshi, do you need any of Clyde's truth serum? We wouldn't be discussing the massacre of those kids if we were in either of our native countries. I wish you continued good fortune. Khodā hāfez

YY: Sayonara, Shahzad.

KO: I hadn't quite left the room yet. If you're still listening Clyde, the parents of the Sandy Hook Newtown massacre sued the conspiracy theorist Alex Jones and won a judgement of $100,000. So who had credibility, Clyde?

CHAPTER TWO

Roberto (KO, as his Zoom companion Dr. Graf, aka Clyde, as he sometimes wished to refer to him) finished his lunch with his wife, Ellie, cleaned up the kitchen, and meandered into his study to exchange thoughts and opinions with other retired, old men in a Zoom chatroom. He was admitted by the host of the day.

SW: No, Mark, my primary care doctor hasn't messaged me yet regarding the MRI findings. It'll probably be in a couple of days.

PM: My aches and pains are primarily a result of my earlier days on the force, when I had to wrestle with some very big, belligerent, drunken guys to cuff them.

KO: How are things in SoCal today, Mark? And how are things in Minnesota, Shahzad?

SW: I'm enjoying my day, Roberto, working on creating an innovative engineering solution for playground equipment for the parks and recreation department here in my city.

PM: Before I go on to answer your latest question, KO, I have some information for Shahzad about a question he asked me yesterday. Remember, you wanted to know what percentage of the guns in the U.S. are owned by gun collectors. As of 2017, about 3 percent of adults own a collection which adds up to about 133 million total guns. That's about 50 percent of the estimated 265 million guns that were owned then by civilians in the U.S. altogether. There are sunny skies in SoCal today, Roberto, and I'm always pleased with the weather.

"

YY: Hi, everyone. I see you're back on the gun topic. That's a lot of guns! What got Americans so interested in having a gun in the first place?

Rx: The straight shooter is in the room, so be careful what you are spewing. Mark, I know you don't claim to be a mathematician; however, when you state that 3 percent of the adult population in the U.S. owns about 50% of all the guns owned by all Americans, it's a little distorted. 3 percent is a little number. Right? Wrong. Actually 3 percent of our adult(18 and older) population is over 8 million people. That's a pretty big number of people.

PM: We have someone who is asking to be "admitted" to our room, so be nice, everyone. Here's the new participant:

??: Excuse me, please. The name of your Zoom chat room is intriguing to me. I don't wish to intrude, so if I am, please tell me and I'll exit. Hello.

PM: You aren't intruding. We're just a bunch of older guys discussing various somewhat controversial topics. My name is Mark. What is yours?

??: I'm Emily Thurmond. I'm in Virginia, and I'm over eighty years old. So, am I qualified to be a participant? I notice, Mark, that the letters in your box are PM and others have YY, KO, and so forth. Are they just initials, or are they monikers?

KO: Yes, Emily, the letters are monikers in a sense. We've placed some of them on each other. Some are actual initials. For example, my letters are KO, but my name is Roberto. However, one of these smart alecks thought of the boxer Roberto Duran, the knockout boxer.

Rx: Ma'am, as you can see, we're all a different gender than you. We're sometimes a bit salty with each other, so beware of that, as well as the fact that there's disagreement in our discussions of the subjects on which we dwell. Currently, we are discussing gun ownership and gun violence in our country.

SW: Hello, Emily. Welcome to Octogenarians Opining. My name is Shahzad. I'm an Iranian American, but my parents were Persian, and I'm a retired civil engineer living in Minnesota. Do you like to go deep into some of the very controversial issues our country is dealing with? We go pretty deep sometimes. For some, it can be a bit boring.

??:   I'm a retired marriage and family counselor. Now I do lots of reading, mostly dealing with popular, controversial issues. If it's all right with all of you, I'd like to stay in the room for a while and see what I can learn, or maybe contribute. By the way, some of you don't look to be in your eighties.

SW: Emily, we have one other gentleman in this room. He's YY or Yoshi. He had just asked an important question before you came into the room. Roberto, since you were a history professor, maybe you can enlighten us as to what brought about so much desire for so many people to wish to possess guns in this country. Did I state your question correctly, Yoshi?

YY: Yes, Shahzad, you did. Thank you. Welcome, Emily. I like your observation.

Rx: I can't resist Emily. What do you think of the ET moniker for you? I don't mean it as an insult since ET's alien status was high above we humanoids.

ET: That would be fine. So, what does the Rx stand for or is it the obvious one?

Rx: I'm Cylde, and I was a pharmacist in Pennsylvania.

KO: Yoshi, I think you and everyone else in this room knows there is a Second Amendment to the Bill of Rights, part of the U.S. Constitution, that gives citizens the right to own guns.

YY: Yes, Roberto, I know that, but why is that amendment in the Constitution? Do most countries have such a provision? It's not in Japan's constitution.

PM: Yoshi, one would have to know the circumstances of the people in the newly created country to fully understand the reasoning and interests of the population back then. Remember, they had taken the colonies away from the British by force not long before they ratified the Constitution.

Rx: Why don't we let the professor give us the lowdown on the whys and wherefores? Go ahead, KO, give us a knockout lecture on the subject.

ET: I can tell you, gentlemen, this much: the 2nd Amendment was originally the thirteenth amendment in Virginia's Bill of Rights before it got to Philadelphia.

KO: Shahzad and Doctor of Pharma, I never had the title of professor, and you know that. However, I'll look into the preceding history of laws allowing gun ownership in the colonies and in England. But it won't be a knockout lecture. Clyde, you'll have to pay for one.

ET: That should be interesting. I can tell you gentlemen this, if you haven't spoken with, or counseled a survivor, friend or family member of a mass shooting, such as the Virginia Tech shooting, it's hard to fully appreciate the devastation gun ownership can have on people's lives.

SW: I apologize, Roberto. I know you were only an "instructor" at a community college. That's still impressive. Emily, speaking of the effects a mass shooting can have on folks, I have been impacted by a mass shooting, but not in a negative way. I was still a college student in 1966 when that Whitman guy went up the 300-foot bell tower at the University of Texas and shot a bunch of people walking around the campus. I became much more involved and interested in my civil engineering major as a result.

YY: I'm sure Mark has spoken to relatives and friends of shooting victims. I told the group before you came into the room, Emily, that one of my business partners was in Las Vegas near the mass shooting there and he was really affected by what he saw and heard.

FT: That's interesting, Yoshi. In what way was he affected?

YY: He told me that he was depleted, drained of energy, and depressed.

PM: Yes, Yoshi, I've experienced my share of speaking to survivors, family members, colleagues, employees, neighbors, you name them, I spoke to them over my years of service. When I was young and a patrolman, sometimes I was the first on the scene. Sometimes people were crying hysterically, screaming, and cussing loudly. It was terrible! By the way, Shahzad, that Whitman guy in the UT bell tower also had a bunch of guns.

YY: Why? Why are all these people driven to kill other people with their guns?

PM: There are a lot of reasons: anger, hate, mental illness, narcotics, especially with the inner city gangs. Maybe Rx, Clyde, can shed some light on the drug addiction problems.

ET: I'd like to interject a comment here. The trauma that many survivors experience is very severe. Not only do they suffer from depression, as Yoshi mentioned, they suffer from many other ailments, some long term. If you would like, I could delve into all the things I've learned from my perspective dealing with patients on this matter.

Rx: I was wondering when one of you guys, Mark, would try to recruit my professionalism into this matter. You know I don't prescribe products in this room; however, I can offer some general information about certain pharmaceuticals and the effects they can have on humans.

KO: Looks like we have lots to talk about in coming Zoom sessions, I'll dig into the historical side of gun ownership rationale and laws. Shahzad is going to tell us how the UT mass shooting incident affected his civil engineering studies and career. Emily can certainly take us into the suffering that results from all these mass shootings and homicides in general. Mark can provide us with some actual experiences he's had dealing with shootings while being a police officer, and Clyde can offer his expert knowledge on drugs and how they can affect humans in a very harmful, criminal way. Okay. I'm going to check out of the room for now. Nice meeting you, Emily. I hope you'll return and be an active participant in this room.

ET: Being on the East Coast, I have to deal with dinner and other matters before most of you. I'm excited about the prospect of some very serious searching for answers to Yoshi's questions.

I'll do my best to make my contribution. to this project you gentlemen have undertaken. So, with that, I'll say "bye."

PM: With Roberto and Emily leaving the room, it's probably a good time for the rest of us to check out of the room. I have to prepare for a presentation I'm giving at a high school in several days regarding what life is like for felons once they are released from prison. It's not a pretty picture. See you guys next Tuesday. Let's exit the room now. Have a great weekend.

Rx: I'm sure, KO, that you want ET in the room. She agrees with you and she's better looking than all of you. Bone up on your arguments, later.

KO: I guess it's time to check out of this session also. Take care, my friends.

SW: Me too. Bye for now Mark and Yoshi. (He waves.)

CHAPTER THREE

It was a Tuesday, and Roberto started collecting his thoughts about 10:30 that morning in preparation for opining again with his friends in the Zoom room. He picked up a couple of internet articles he had printed related to the history, laws, and culture of gun ownership in the United States and reread the lines he had underlined when first reading the articles. At 2:00 p.m. MDT, he clicked the link to join the others.

Rx: As a pharmacist in business, I didn't mind terribly that some folks consumed far too many medications. If there were significant possible side effects, we would tell the customer. Info and instructions also came with the meds.

YY: The instructions and side effects information is usually in such small, light print that they're very difficult to read.

KO: It looks like we have a new subject to discuss today. I came prepared to talk about the rationale and history of gun ownership in this country.

PM: Hi everyone, glad you guys are still alive and your minds are still functioning.

Rx: There's always a guy who believes he is a comedian who shows up sooner or later on his own.

ET: Good afternoon, gentlemen. I hope all of you enjoyed your weekend. Since we have a serious topic to discuss, I've been finding all sorts of highly informative information to discuss with you besides my own experiences.

Rx: We might have bit off more than we can chew with the alien coming into this room.

PM: Now who's attempting to mimic a comedian?

SW: Sweet afternoon, everyone. I'm a bit late because I've been trying to find thought's about what I can contribute to our topic. I'm a bit stressed because I've forgotten things I used to know well. So, be gentle with this old guy today, please…

YY: As some of us have said numerous times over the months we've been chatting together, we are having problems remembering everything we knew and experienced. What do you wish to tell us, Emily?

ET: I'll try to avoid Clyde's rude epithet and get to the substance of my thoughts. During my years of practice, I did counsel family members and friends of victims of mass shootings, but I never counseled anyone related to a mass shooter. I've been looking at Charles Whitman lately because Shahz brought up that name and the terrible shooting incident. If we look closely at the shooters themselves, we may determine that they are also victims before those shootings. Of course, some inflict death on themselves after shooting.

Rx: You are beginning to sound like what some people call a "bleeding heart liberal." How can you sympathize with a mass murderer?

KO: Since our newest member brought up the Virginia Tech shooting, I got curious about that shooter, a student named Seung -Hui Cho. He also had a troubled life.

SW: Emily, I hope you can enlighten us more about Whitman and Roberto, how was this Cho guy's life troubled more than everyone's life in general?

Rx: KO and ET, are you two trying to enlist us in feeling sorry for these mass killers? KO, how about your curiosity for those who were killed?

SW: Clyde, you can sure find fault with others pretty easily. My dad used to quote Rumi, a Sufi Muslim, who said, "In seeing other people's faults, we ourselves then commit a fault." In the Western world, that's probably called "judging." Emily, would you mind telling us some of what you discovered about Whitman?

ET: Shahzad, you are a good spirit. Here's a little of what I read about Charles Whitman. His mom divorced his dad because he was physically and emotionally abusive to her and their children. Charles drove from Texas to Florida to get his mother away from his dad safely. He even enlisted a police officer's help in protecting his mom while she packed her belongings. Charles was a Marine, where he probably learned how to shoot well, although he was court-martialed for having a personal firearm on base, as well as other infractions. He married a teacher and was a scout leader for a while. Obviously, he was acceptable to the Marine recruiters and the woman he married. At one point, he abused amphetamines and experienced bad headaches. So far, one can realize that Charles grew up in an unhealthy home. He was not a good Marine, used drugs inappropriately, yet he had compassion for his mother. If you wish to learn more about what got him to where he was on the day of the shooting, I'll be pleased to tell you more.

Rx: ET, you haven't persuaded me that he was any more a victim than millions of our fellow Americans. Shahzad, I wasn't judging nor finding fault, as Rumi pondered, just making an observation and kindly offering a suggestion. No harm in doing that, is there? I'm sure Rumi wouldn't find fault with that.

PM: You probably all know how bad it is for single mothers raising boys in the inner cities of this country and all the problems with crime those boys can have. Yet equally, or maybe more harmful to kids, is raising them in unhealthful households where fathers or mothers are very abusive, especially physically and emotionally abusive, in front of their kids If you've watched that TV show, Dr. Phil McGraw, read any Dear Abby–type advice columns, talked to any social worker, police officer, school counselor, or marriage and family counselor like Emily, you'd know just how impactful this is on crime, gun violence, and mental health in general in this country.

YY: Roberto, you brought back that Virginia Tech mass shooter, so did he grow up in an unhealthful household with a physically or emotionally abusive parent like that Whitman fellow did? By the way, just in case any of you remember I was waiting for my MRI results. I got them. I have some torn muscle tissue in my left shoulder area, so first my physician wants me to go through some physical therapy and hopefully I won't have to deal with surgery or painkillers. I just want to get back on the golf courses with my friends.

KO: Thanks for following up on my comment about that VT shooter, Yoshi. From everything I've read so far, his family didn't bring him up in an unhealthful way. When he was eight years old, his parents immigrated from South Korea. When he was in middle school, he was diagnosed with a severe anxiety disorder, with selective mutism and a major depressive disorder. He was unable to interact with classmates and teachers verbally most of the time. This kid was mentally ill and never got the necessary treatment he needed to be a functioning person. I'll give you more details later.

Rx: Now we have a third cause of the development of a mass shooter. Does anyone else have a fourth pretext, excuse me, I mean cause? KO, a good psychiatrist would have prescribed selective serotonin reuptake inhibitors and sent Cho on his way. Oops, I prescribed medication. Damn it.

YY: Thanks Roberto for giving us that information. I know some kids coming from other countries without knowing English before coming, are pretty hesitant trying to speak English in front of regular English speaking people. They don't want to get laughed at for mispronouncing a word or using the wrong word. Emily, is it that easy to treat those disorders as easy as Clyde says?

ET: Yoshi, I'm not a psychiatrist nor a pharmacist. As counselors and therapists, we don't prescribe drugs as treatments. However, some doctors probably would disagree with Clyde's simplistic solution. Mental health is complex.

PM: Shahzad, a couple of days ago you said something about the bell tower building having an influence on what kind of engineering you studied. That has stuck with me. Would you like to elaborate?

YY: Yeah, Shahzad, you decided to study civil engineering because something about that building stimulated you to learn about buildings?

SW: Thanks for remembering what I mentioned. I'd rather not get too far off our primary subject of gun violence right now. Let me just say that for Whitman to see that building in a way the architects and contractors designed and built it, Whitman's purpose in using that bell tower was totally different from theirs.

PM: It's amazing how distorted some people's thinking is when it comes to crime. Both schools we've been talking about were places for young people to live and study on those campuses, but for Whitman and Cho, they were killing fields. We've got guys going into supermarkets, movie theaters, hotels and all sorts of worksites to take other people's lives. It's very sickening, and as a former law enforcement officer, I am much more concerned these days about mass shootings than I ever was twenty or thirty years ago. For a ten-year period in the '90s and early 2000s, semiautomatic gun sales were banned.

YY: Why was that ban lifted?

PM: When President Clinton signed it, the ban was to be just ten years long. Roberto, do you want to provide more history of the ban?

KO: Mark, I know the ban was part of a major crime bill Congress passed in 1994. Crime was just escalating, and people wanted Washington to do more about it. Some of it had to do with illegal drugs and associated crimes. Also, some wanted to stop the sale of the Russian-made AK-47s. However, by 2004, with Bush being president, the ban expired amid debate over its success. With so many semiautomatic guns in this country, it was hard to determine if the ban was effective.

ET: Thanks, gentlemen,for another stimulating conversation. It's nice getting to know all of you and having you share your knowledge, experience, and curiosity. I'm learning a lot. But for now, I must exit this room. Goodbye.

YY: Hope to hear about those survivors of mass shootings you have treated over the years. I'll be back on Thursday. Cheers!

ET: Yes, Yoshi, I'll share some of my experiences with you in the days to come.

Rx: My prescription to you Zoomers is to get off this topic and go have some fun.

CHAPTER FOUR

Thursday came about so quickly, like most days in Roberto's life now. He rushed to the Plaza de Las Cruces to buy a birthday gift for his granddaughter, Tina, that he found on her gift registry. He had a quick lunch and went to his office, got on his computer, and Zoomed with his fellow octogenarians.

ET: Yes, we may get a lot of rain from that storm.

Rx: It's not yet hurricane season, and you're already expecting a big storm coming your way.

KO: Buenos tardes, everyone. We could use some rain here.

PM: If you think you need rain, you should come to Arizona, Nevada or California. Getting on to our more serious topic, I read in the newspaper recently that an eighteen-year-old girl on a first date with a nineteen-year-old boy was shot and killed in a movie theater here in SoCal. A twenty-year-old guy, who was first in another theater in the complex with some other guys, went into the couple's theater, aimed his gun in that nearly empty theater, and shot both teenagers in the head, execution-style. The shooter told police that he had been diagnosed with schizophrenia and hadn't taken his medication for a while. Emily, that is a clear case of mental illness as the initial and primary problem.

ET: How awful for those two teenagers and their families and friends. Yes, that is one of the mental health illnesses of individuals who commit murder. Did the shooter tell the police why he selected those two young people to shoot?

KO: I heard something about that shooting. The young man who was killed was a popular high school soccer star named Barajas. Didn't the other guys with the shooter know he had a gun with him?

PM: No, the shooter didn't know the teenagers he killed. Roberto, his three friends abandoned him when he started acting strangely. They wondered what he had in a bag at one point. The three friends thought the shooter did have a gun. They left the theater without him. They were in the parking lot when they saw him run out of the theater and get into his car.

Rx: Mark, are you trying to write a police report on a shooting. You're sure getting meticulous with all of this information. What's your point?

PM: Mental illness is often the underlying factor in why someone perpetrates a crime, especially shootings. We need to focus on mental illness as much as we focus our attention on guns.

KO: I know mental illness has become the focus of our discussions lately, but I'd like to suggest we return to another aspect of the topic on guns, one that Clyde assigned and Yoshi mentioned several days back: the history behind the Second Amendment to our U.S. Constitution. Do you want to learn some of it now?

Rx: Yeah, KO, I'd like to get off the mental illness obsession for now. Go ahead, give us your finest lecture on why that amendment is in the Constitution. I believe I already know, but go ahead, you can have the floor.

YY: Yes, Roberto, I remember asking about the reasons for that amendment and whether other countries also have one in their constitutions.

KO: Emily, Mark and Shahzad, I hope it's ok with you as well. I'll try to be brief. Yoshi, I'll answer the second questions first. There are only three countries in the world that provide their citizens, in their constitutions, a right to keep and bear arms: Guatemala, Mexico and the U.S. Most of you would probably guess that there isn't any date for its historical beginning; however, we know it began well over a thousand years ago. Of course, back then the arms weren't guns. It is thought to have its origins in Clyde's ancestry, in Germanic tribes; some came west to the British Isles. In England, rulers differed from other European countries whose rulers had standing armies and began to rely on the peasantry to maintain their control and defend them. I read an article on the internet that stated that with this change came a significant evolution of political systems in England. The peasants, or citizens, of England could be called upon to use their arms to defend a king. That seemed to be a very good reason to let folks keep and bear arms in their homes. As a result, under Henry I, Britain became a bit democratic. Henry II, in 1181, declared that all British citizens between fifteen and sixty were required to purchase and keep arms.

Rx: Excuse me, KO, I didn't realize how minute your lecture was going to be. Can we take a short break from it and return to it later? Please!

SW: I was just getting into it, Roberto. It's fascinating how this concept evolved.

KO: Yes, Clyde, we can take a break from it. I thought all of you would really appreciate just how far back the notion of keeping and bearing arms went.

ET: Yes, Roberto, I appreciate your efforts to inform us and the longevity and purpose of the concept.

VY: I've got another question for Emily, Mark, or anyone else who wishes to offer an answer. Why is it that it seems that only the male gender is involved in mass shootings? It also seems that these males are usually pretty young.

PM: Emily, I'm sure you'll have something to say about Yoshi's question, but I'd just like to offer a quick answer. Since we have been discussing this topic, I've been checking out some of the latest data and statistics. Regarding the question, the male gender has been responsible for about 98 percent since 1966. Remember that year? That's when. What's his name?.. Whitman, Whitman shot people from the Bell Tower.

SW: One of the things I was going to say more in depth is how people can misappropriate something and use it for very different purposes. That tower was the heart of the campus. The bells and clock had a specific purpose. Other than the school president's office, most of the 27 floors were used as a library, yet Whitman only saw in his distorted mind, the Bell Tower as a place to shoot from. Can you imagine the Wright brothers ever dreaming that someone would think of using an airplane to jump from and parachute back to the ground? Sorry. When you said Bell Tower it triggered the civil engineer in me.

ET: We need spontaneity at times, Shahzad. Regarding the male gender and violence, this is a cultural and social creation that dates back to the days when men were the hunters for food. Men have, in most societies and cultures, been the dominant sex. Look at Roberto's findings: kings were in charge. It wasn't until Elizabeth I that England actually had a woman as the true monarch. It was the men who were in the standing armies in European countries and the Roman Empire. So, is it any surprise that the male gender is inured to a weapon that can kill many people in one episode?

YY: Thanks, Emily and Mark, for being so informative.

Rx: I probably shouldn't have interrupted KO's boring lecture. I had no idea this tangent yakety yak was to take us on.

KO: Ha, Ha, Clyde, be careful what you ask for. Yoshi, those were good questions.

SW: Before we get back to Roberto's informative lecture, I'd like to ask Emily or anyone else, this somewhat naive and perhaps insurmountable question: Is there anything that can be done to erase, delete, radically change the social and cultural inclinations that were instilled in the male gender so that we can reduce the need and desire for weapons in that gender?

Rx: Brainwashing! Have them watch CNN or MSNBC all day, maybe that would do it.

ET: Shahzad, that's a powerful question - one that's probably challenged minds for as long as there have been weapons used to kill other humans. Unfortunately, parents, relatives, and the greater society instill into the subjective minds of very young kids, by the age of six, usually, all kinds of notions that later have an unconsciously controlling impact on their thoughts, instincts and emotions in later life. I'll see what else I can offer you for more substantive insight.

PM: I'll tell you, Shahzad, what did it for me. In the 1950s, not long after my parents bought our first TV set, my brothers and I started watching TV shows like *The Lone Ranger*, Roy Rogers, Gene Autry, and other Western shows. Those guys guy were all heroes, the good guys, and they were all good with their pistols. Lots of people got shot in the TV shows and movies I've seen.

KO: I'm sure those shows had some effect on boys back then, but what, as Shahzad's question covers, explains why police officers shoot and kill unarmed Black boys and men so often in our country? I don't think the Long Ranger would do that. Are you ready for me to get back to my boring/informative lecture?

YY: Yes, please do.

SW: ditto that!

KO: The weapon of choice under King Edward I was the longbow, the crossbow, so it was owned by all citizens used even in fighting in France and elsewhere. The four Edwards, and English kings after them, had to deal with the rules of the Magna Carta of 215 that gave barons more influence in ruling their turfs. Under Edward IV, every Englishman or Irishman had to own a bow equal to his height. I wonder how that would work with some of the NBA players. The only restrictions on carrying your longbow around were if it was used for some criminal assault or taken into areas where it was prohibited to go, the King's court, etc. In the sixteenth century, firearms were invented and could be carried around. The French government under Maximilian imposed a ban on the manufacturing and sale of firearms at that time. In 1514, in England, Henry VIII placed a ban on carrying and possessing pistols. In the 1540s, Henry had to relinquish his laws restricting owning and carrying firearms. Under Elizabeth I, the concept of a militia brought about armed civilians who could be used to protect her reign and the country. Under King Charles I, Parliament wanted to be in control of the militia and…

Rx: Excuse me again, Professor, but wasn't it about that time that Englishmen had intruded themselves onto the eastern shores of what is now Virginia and Massachusetts? I hope see-saw and yakety yak don't take on more tangents.

KO: Yes, doctor, Englishmen, with guns, were on Roanoke Island as early as 1585.

ET: You're correct, Roberto, but as a Virginian, I must say that those left on Roanoke Island were never seen again. It wasn't until 1607, when over a one hundred men and boys were left at what became Jamestown, that the English had a permanent settlement in what is now the United States.

RX: Okay, okay, let's get back to England so the professor can finish his lecture.

KO: Well, Parliament and Charles both wanted to be in control of the militia, and as a result a standing army led by Oliver Cromwell embarked on a civil war. As more and more Englishmen immigrated to Virginia, Massachusetts and other places in North America, the colonists carried on their lives with the culture they had grown up with in England. All men had guns to protect their families and their settlements, but they didn't have them to keep the king in power, as had been the situation in much of English history. Following Cromwell's military dictatorship, Charles II and then James II ruled, and in 1689 a Bill of Rights was created in England that allowed Protestant religious members to keep and bear arms. There was a British attempt to disarm Americans in 1774, as they could see a revolution flashing before their eyes. In Virginia, George Washington and George Mason are given a lot of credit for writing the thirteenth amendment to Virginia's Bill of Rights, which allows citizens the right to keep and bear arms. That was written in 1776. That right was installed in the U.S. Constitution in the Bill of Rights as Amendment II in 1789, with the help of Mason and James Madison. Well, students, that's the sequence of events over many hundreds of years that now allows citizens in the U.S. to keep and bear arms, and why so many of our citizens have that need so ingrained in them.

YY: Thank you, Roberto. It is more understandable why so many Americans feel the need to possess a firearm.

SW: Weren't the Spanish on the West Coast with their guns at the same time?

KO: Well, Shahzad, they were exploring in the area of California then, but they didn't actually create a settlement like Jamestown until over a hundred years later. They were busy conquering what is now the land of Mexico.

Rx: Enough, enough with the history for me today. Auf Wiedersehen!

PM: Obviously, it was very necessary for every home to have a rifle back then. When would you say that it became much less necessary for citizens to own guns in this country? Please let me know your answer next Tuesday. Bye, all.

CHAPTER FIVE

Mark wasn't going to have time for his lunch since he had just gotten home from an appointment with Doctor M, his ophthalmologist, twenty miles west of his home in Claremont. He was glad to receive another "stable" report regarding his macular degeneration eyesight issue, but he also wanted to get online to chat with his fellow eighty-plus-year-old friends, since it had been four days since doing so. He got an apple, went into his den, plopped down in front of his recently purchased all-in-one desktop computer, and entered the Zoom chatroom.

VY: Yes, Clyde, I'm a member of the Oak Creek Golf Cub. However, I'm not as active golfing as I used to be because of my shoulder injury issue, but I love my social life with the members there. Do you golf much?

ET: That golf club must be pretty darn expensive to be a member of, Yoshi.

Rx: Yes, I golf some, but now I have to be careful with my swings so as not to cause pain in my upper back, my traps. I don't belong to a club any longer.

YY: Yes, Emily, it's kind of expensive for most folks. It's about $10,000. annually.

KO: I see you guys have changed the topic on me again.

El: No, Roberto, we were all awaiting your entrance to stimulate us us further in discussion about firearms violence in this country. Although I could offer some of my experiences treating patients who had loved ones or friends who were victims of someone with a gun.

Rx: This chatroom is beginning to feel like the classroom of Prof. KO.

SW: Hi, everyone. I'd really like hearing about your professional experiences.

KO: Yes, please do, Emily.

ET: Well, it seems that I got a couple of votes. Quite a few years ago now, in 2007, following the Virginia Tech mass shooting, a student there came in for therapy due to the stress of not being able to function hardly at all. Her dearest friend, from elementary school on, was a victim of that mass shooting. They weren't in in the same area when Seung-Hui Cho emptied his guns on students. She, Pam, and her friend, Jane, were both in their senior year at VT. The friend was one of the thirty-two killed that day. Pam, even though she lived on campus with Jane, drove home to be with her parents that night. Pam cried all night and felt that a big, dark hole in her heart and life had suddenly been created. She didn't know how she would ever be able to manage her life without Jane in it. The stress got to be unbearable by the next morning. Her mother tried to comfort her, but all she could do was cry. She couldn't eat anything; she just stayed in bed all that day and thought about Jane. After a couple of weeks of this nonfunctioning behavior, and upon numerous suggestions from family members and friends, Pam made an appointment to get counseling for her debilitating stage of grief.

ET: She came to see me for help. After a few visits, with her crying spells and recounting her feelings for Jane, she decided the therapy wasn't helping her. She couldn't see that she was a survivor and didn't have to be a victim, like Jane was, of this terrible, traumatic event. Let's take a breather from my recounting this for a few moments before Clyde requests it.

PM: I had to deal with people like Pam, either injured or uninjured, following a shooting incident. We had to obtain as much information as we could from folks like Pam in order to gather evidence and arrest the perpetrator. It was very hard because these folks are very fragile soon after the incident. We had to give way to their sobbing and emotions, try to console them when possible. Their feelings are very deep, and empathy and sympathy are called for.

Rx: I bet you were a great consoler when you were a wet-behind-the-ears rookie patrolman.

KO: Clyde, Mark's trying to tell us about his challenging experiences. It's nothing to make fun of. Police officers have to deal with these terrible situations every day in this country. That's why we must dig deeper and discover ideas to diminish gun violence in our nation.

SW: So, Emily, how does a person who has survived gun violence get over the emptiness, depression, anxiety, et cetera, to go on with their lives?

ET: It's not easy, and for some it takes a good deal of time. Pam came back to see me several months later. She was in a better place, but not out of the woods yet. Some of her other friends worked to involve her in doing little things, like volunteering to paint a house for an elderly woman. She was also able to meet with some of Jane's classmates who were shot and survived and others who were near Jane at the time. That helped her bond with those students.

Rx: Without question, there have been many other reasons for Americans to own guns to protect themselves. On the western border, pioneers had to deal with the savages, slave owners still had to keep their slaves under control and there were bandits to deal with. But then came the Civil War, and most Southerners surely needed guns for protection. Nowadays, we law-abiding citizens need guns to protect us from burglars, carjackers, protesters, and maybe the government. Who knows?

PM: Yes, Clyde, you have some good points there. However, we do have something that we didn't have back in the early or mid-1800s: we have a very professional system of law enforcement, with police and sheriff's departments in almost every city in the country, that do a lot of the protecting you are referring to. One couldn't make a 911 call back then and have someone come to you within minutes.

Rx: Wait a minute, Mark! I don't think we are living in the same universe, let alone the same country. In my country, a cop named Derek Chauvin pressed a knee on the neck of a guy named George Floyd in Minneapolis for nine minutes, thus killing him. Is this the professional system you're speaking of? Or how about when many thousands took to the streets all across this, my country, with many of them not protesting Floyd's death but looting stores and burning buildings, including police department buildings? Where was the law-enforcement system then?

PM: That was a terrible time. Chauvin was tried and convicted of his crime. Yes, lots of people took to the streets to protest before Chauvin was tried, and they protested loudly. But the people who looted and burned buildings were criminals, not protesters, and many were arrested, and some are still being sought. Unfortunately, things got very political, with some folks wanting to defund the police and change some laws that protect police officers from certain liabilities. As a result, some officers retired early and others left their forces. It has been more difficult to recruit new officers. Some changes are necessary for the system to serve communities better. I agree with that.

Rx: You're not going to convince me that things are getting better regarding crime. I just read an article today about crime in Milwaukee, Wisconsin. It is experiencing the worst crime and violence in recorded history, a 93 percent increase from 2019. Where is this professional law-enforcement system in that city? Hiding under a rock?

PM: Clyde, one can always find a story like that at any time and in any place. However, let me provide you with some of the circumstances in that city and around the country. As I said previously, some police departments have lost many members of their forces. The pandemic caused a major disruption in most Americans' lives. More guns were purchased, about 23 million, or about a 60 percent increase, and stolen during the protesting, and with schools closed and businesses closed and jobs lost, many young men had a lot of time on their hands to hang out, use drugs, and cause trouble.

YY: If I can butt in here for a comment, I'd like to follow up on something Mark said last week. He was talking about the influence TV shows had on him and other boys in the 1950s. Well, I've read that several TV shows this fall are about serial killers. Shows like Dexter: New Blood and Chucky are available for boys and young men to be influenced by them. Why does society allow such sick shows to be shown on national TV? What kind of person enjoys this stuff?

Rx: FREEDOM! Yoshi.

SW: Mark, you mentioned the large increase in gun sales last year. Well, is this coincidental or just by chance? According to the FBI chief, a guy named Wray, homicides increased in 2020 by 30 percent, the greatest increase in the U.S. since the Bureau started collecting this data. Clyde, do you have an explanation for this correlation between gun sales increasing and homicides also increasing? Is that just FREEDOM? Other countries don't have that freedom and they're safer.

Rx: Yes, see-saw, it can be explained. You and the others just wish to look at the problems with guns, but there are other explanations for why the homicide rate increased. A week or two ago, one of you wise guys asked me about drugs. Well, I'm ready to give you a lesson on the drug situation in our country if you are willing to listen and learn.

KO: I am, Clyde. Please give us your pharmaceutical knowledge of drug use in the U.S.

ET: I'm alert and ready to listen, Dr. Pharmacist.

Rx: I'm going to assume yakety-yak and see-saw will consent to listen to my presentation. Well, students, probably most of you have a mild addiction, as most folks do. Since there is no substance involved, these are more like cravings or habits, such as watching certain TV shows, especially sports for a lot of men. Some people need to play with their smartphones all day or listen to podcasts all the time. Some are more serious habits or weaknesses, such as sexual ones, like the need for porn all the time. Most adults in the U.S. are addicted to legal addictive substances, drugs, like caffeine in coffee, tea, sodas, and even chocolate. Then there are smokers who get addicted to nicotine, which is the leading cause of preventable deaths. Now, drugs that I sold in my pharmacy each had a medical purpose for the purchaser and user. You've probably heard their names, and maybe you've used some to sleep, relieve pain, or whatever. Let's see, there's Valium for sleeping, anxiety, and so on; opioids for pain relief, which are easy to get hooked on; and Ritalin, Ambien, Adderall, and many more. Now, as you know, lots of scummy people didn't come to my pharmacy with a doctor's prescription to treat a medical issue; they bought their drugs on the black market. Of course, those drugs are illegal.

ET: Excuse me, Clyde, I'd like to interject some info at this point. Speaking of legal drugs, which can cause addictions, the United States pharmaceutical industry is the largest in the world. In 2015, its sales were $263 billion, and by 2020 they were over $306 billion. Lots of medical doctors attend lots of workshops sponsored by pharmaceutical companies. When a patient complains of pain, often a doctor will prescribe a drug, like an opioid, for relief. Many doctors haven't studied how food nutrition can keep one healthy. Sorry for the interruption, Clyde and all.

Rx: Your statement was unworthy of interrupting my pertinent information, but I have a forgiving heart. All of you, I'm sure, have heard of many of the most infamous illegal drugs. Marijuana is legal in some states but illegal in others. Obviously, it is pretty benign compared with the other widely used illegal drugs. However, if you get addicted to cannabis as a teen, you may lose some of your IQ by the time you're our age. Heroin, which is an opioid, has claimed many users who started with legal opioids to kill pain. Over 10,000 a year in the U.S. die from overdosing on this drug. Another dangerous illegal drug is meth, short for methamphetamine, which can make you come alive and very active. Crystal is popular in bars, etc. Then there's crack cocaine, or crack rock, which is smoked. It can give the user a high and lots of energy for a short time.

SW: Pardon me, Clyde, may I ask you a worthy question? Why are these drugs illegal? It seems as though they have some advantages.

Rx: Yes, see-saw, I mean, Shahzad, yours is a worthy inquiry. If a drug has no medical purpose for consumption, a doctor has no reason for prescribing it, and a pharmacy has no reason for providing it to a customer. Addicts of these drugs are really harming the functioning of their brains. As you can see, there are many addicted people in our country. Just wanting to please your taste buds can make you addicted to some sugary foods. Some boys and men don't control their testosterone hormones and become sex addicts and abuse others, as you know. PM can probably educate us more on how illegal drugs are sold on the black market in urban areas, with a lot of gun violence involved. Right, Commander?

YY: It seems, from what you have explained, Clyde, that we all have either very bad habits or addictions to one thing or another, whether they involve drugs in various forms, eating disorders, sex, or social media. It seems to be easy for us to get hooked on something. What's going to be the future for our grand- and great-grandchildren with all these addictions being so prevalent?

ET: That's a good question, Yoshi. The answers can be quite scary!

KO: Doctor Graf, before Commander Jackson gives us the lowdown on illegal drug trafficking in this country, I want to tell you that I take offense, and I've told you previously, at your derogatory name-calling of Mr. Iravani, "see-saw," or Mr. Yanamoto, "yakety yak," or even Commander Jackson, "PM." These men are all distinguished, and you should show them respect. Commander Mark Jackson was awarded the Medal of Valor by the Pasadena Police Department for saving people's lives. Shahzad Iravani donated his time to develop some plans for the Army Corps of Engineers to help redevelop the levees in New Orleans to withstand a Category 5 hurricanes. And Yoshi Yanamoto got some of his real estate investment partners to set up a scholarship program for students at the University of California, Irvine, and together they donated millions of dollars. So again, I advocate for them and for the respect they deserve.

ET: Wow! I had no idea how distinguished you gentlemen are. Congratulations on your fantastic achievements!

PM: We've sure covered a lot of ground today. I appreciate Roberto's history lesson and Clyde's presentation on legal and illegal drugs, along with the rest of the commentary from all of you. I'll accept Clyde solicitation to offer some info and perhaps my point of view from my experience as a police officer dealing with drug trafficking in the near future. But for now, I'm going to leave the room so I can eat the delicious meal my wife is preparing for me. With that, I hope to see you folks Thursday afternoon.

Rx: Professor Alvarez, I don't appreciate your denunciation of my kidding around with you guys. That's how a lot of older guys talk in my community: we tease the hell out of each other. The teasing is not meant to be derogatory; it's companionship and camaraderie. So, maybe, Roberto you should dismount your high-horse opinionating. KO, just lighten up a little so we can all get along.

ET: Excuse me, gentlemen. Clyde, have you ever asked Yoshi and Shahzad how they feel about your "good old boys, locker room" teasing? Perhaps they should speak up if it offends them. Obviously, Roberto, you do respect those men as well as Mark, and you don't like the teasing directed at you either. Too much of this rancor can ruin our intentions of developing some sort of solution to reduce gun violence. I'm sure most of us need to think about dinner as Mark is. Good evening, all.

SW: Clyde, you seem a lot like some of the Fox News hosts, the ones that have ugly nicknames, especially regarding the President, for people they don't like. I don't really understand why you refer to me as "see-saw." Good evening everyone.

YY: Let's not get into the O.K. Corral. Remember, we don't want gun violence. We want to end it.

CHAPTER SIX

Emily had been conscious of the time all day. She had participated in a Zoom session with some other retired marriage and family counselors in the morning. She actually told the group about her participation in Octogenarians Opining and about the topic being discussed. Several of the others became very interested and wanted to know more about what specifically was being discussed. By four o'clock Eastern Time, she was revved up and anxious to enter the Zoom chatroom.

KO: Yes, I think it would be a very valuable improvement to our education system. Kids just don't reach a level of competence, skills, and knowledge in K–12 grades in order to enter the workforce these days. Two additional years of trade school or community college would be a real asset to employers and students. So yes, Mark, I'd definitely support a plan for minimal or no costs for the students.

ET: Good afternoon, gentlemen. It sounds like we're discussing increased education today. I'm all for it. Looking back on my own education, I now wish I would have persevered in school until I earned a PhD. in psychology.

PM: When the others sign on this afternoon, I can offer some information on the illegal drug trafficking crisis in this country, the associated gun violence, and a bit about police tactics in dealing with the problem. I'm sure you two already are well aware of much of what I have to say.

ET: In my practice, as you know, I've had numerous patients who had been prescribed medication for pain relief, only to be hooked on the drug over time and become drug addicts. The addiction caused families to split up, jobs to be lost, and in some cases, especially with opioids, death.

Rx: You're talking about drugs without me, the pharmacist, being in the room. How could you!?

KO: Hi, Clyde. Lighten up. Mark, as you probably heard, is prepared to give his talk.

SW: Good afternoon, friends. I hope you are all well and in an agreeable mood this afternoon. It's actually been raining here in St. Paul. Have I missed anything of significance yet?

PM: No, Shahzad, you haven't, unless you classify Clyde's burst that we mentioned drugs before he, a pharmacist, entered the room.

YY: Hi, everyone. It's a beautiful sunny day in SoCal - great for golfing. What's up?

KO: Now that we are all present, it would be an opportune time for Commander Jackson to inform us of what he knows about illegal drug trafficking and the associated gun violence in our country. Mark, are you ready to dive in?

PM: Yes, Roberto. I'll try to respect Clyde's request for brevity; however, there's a lot of information to cover. Since the United States has the most consumers of many Illegal drugs, international drug trafficking is focused on this country. It's a very lucrative business. In 2016, Americans spent about $150 billion on cocaine, heroin, and methamphetamines. These drugs mostly come from a few countries: heroin and opium and now fentanyl from Afghanistan; cocaine from Colombia, Peru, and Bolivia; and meth comes mostly from Mexican cartels. Am I taking too much of your time yet, Clyde? Illegal drugs get into this country via several means, and traffickers are always trying new methods. The Mexican drug cartels can smuggle illegal drugs into our country over, under, and around walls and fences. They have lots of money and resources to acquire many ways to do so. Most of the stuff from Mexico comes through the ports of entry in cars and trucks. Just think of this: over 14 million cars and trucks enter the US at the San Diego port of entry every year. There are 330 ports of entry on the border. By far, most illicit drugs come across the southern border, but are conveyed by ships and air traffic.

Rx: You're going to make me snooze if this rambling continues. You haven't connected all this information to gun violence yet.

YY: Please, Clyde, don't interrupt Mark's report now. We need to learn about the domestic drug trafficking and the gun violence associated with it.
Please continue, Mark.

KO: You've got my vote, Mark.

PM: Okay, I hope I can keep Clyde awake for a few more minutes. Cartels have created primary drug marketing regions in our country. They have corridors—interstate highways, etc. - through which the drugs are transported to distribution centers. Obviously, big cities like Chicago, New York, Houston, Detroit, and several others are the best markets. These drugs are then distributed and sold by street gangs, motorcycle gangs, and prison gangs. Some gangs operate on a national level.

Rx: Mark, where are the guns??? Why are so many drug-dealing gangs killing each other? Where do they get their guns? What percentage of all homicides in the US are

directly related to illegal drug sales? drug sales? What are the DEA and ATF statistics?
Put some meat on the bones.

ET: Clyde, shush! Let Mark's unfolding of his comprehensive message of info flow without your constant interruptions, please. Thank you.

PM: Here's a stunning statistic, Clyde. In 2005, the federal government reported a survey that concluded that 800,000 teenagers between the ages of 12 and 17 sold illegal drugs within the past year. Another fact to illustrate just how powerful the Mexican cartels are: in 2008, the U.S. created a project to help Mexican soldiers take on the cartels with better equipment, including helicopters and surveillance technology, with a budget of one billion four hundred million dollars. Even with this extra help, the cartels were able to outgun and outnumber the army.

Rx: It seems the alien has come out of her spaceship and has taken on a negative assertiveness that is bordering on controlling our dialogue.

SW: I had no idea the Mexican cartels were so strong and pervasive in our country and Mexico. How can our government successfully defeat them?

PM: Let's take L.A., for instance. It has the largest number of gang members in the U.S. The Mexican cartels can be wholesalers to these street gangs, which then handle the retail distribution of drugs on the streets. Each gang, whether Hispanic, Black, or Asian, mostly has its own designated turf to distribute within. Most of the turf is in disadvantaged, poverty-level neighborhoods. The gang violence with guns Isn't necessarily due to drug trafficking. The drug dealers want to make money, not go to prison or get killed in a shootout. The gun violence is mostly committed by young guys under twenty-four in the barrios and neighborhoods of the inner cities. These young guys commit crimes to get money to buy guns from burglars and low-level gun dealers. Chicago police, in 2017, were able to collect over 7,000 guns from gang members. Obviously, handguns and even semi-automatic rifles are easy to obtain illegally. There are about 30,000 gangs in the U.S., and they're responsible for about 2,000 gun related homicides annually, most in big cities, but some in suburbs, small towns, and rural areas. Of all homicides last year, almost half involved Black victims, and males made up over 14,000 victims compared to 3,500 females.

YY: All along, I thought the big-time drug dealing gangs in big inner-city areas were responsible for all the killings, and I thought the number was greater than 2,000.

SW: That was my understanding too, having read and heard lots of reporting in my newspapers and on TV. Why can't the FBI, DEA, the ATF, or the military go after the Mexican cartels, repel them, and put them out of business in our country?

Rx: PM, I mean Commander, you seem to be saying the drug cartels, being more like entrepreneurs, are more or less innocuous when it comes to gun violence. Am I getting that right? I understand some of those thugs, punks, addicts, and criminals in street gangs wish to be pharmacists by creating crystal meth, which is popular in bars and nightclubs. I had to obtain degrees to do that.

PM: Gentlemen, I didn't mean to characterize the Mexican cartels as being nonviolent. They are very violent in Mexico. They are responsible for thousands of deaths. Of course, those cartels fight for turf in our country as well, but with much less visibility and violence. The DEA has a list of at least six cartels with large operating areas in the U.S. I think you can see the picture clearly. If we didn't have so many drug addicts in our country, the cartels wouldn't be able to do much business and domestic gangs wouldn't be distributing so many drugs and the homicide rate would be lower. And, of course, if guns weren't so readily available, there would be fewer homicides.

Rx: There's a bit of sophistry in your argument against guns. If there were fewer people, there would probably be fewer homicides also.

KO: Doctor, I think Mark is trying to give us the truth. You think if a country has less population, the gun homicides would also be fewer. With your logic, a country with 40 percent of the population of the U.S. would look like this: U.S. homicides in 2015 were about 16,000. Forty percent of that figure is about 6,400. Well, let me see, Japan has a population of around 126 million, or just below 40 percent of our population. In 2016, that country experienced about 344 homicides. If Japan had our population, it would have had about 860 homicides. Is that sophistry, Doctor?

VY: Mark, or perhaps Emily, is there anything besides living in poverty, fatherless households, less-than-good schools, and bad neighborhoods that caused so many minority boys to become drug addicts, gang members, and, in some cases, killers? Is that why Hispanics and Blacks make up the majority of the male prison population in this country? Is it basically a socioeconomic inequity that is the underlying factor?

RX: Yakety Yak, excuse me please, Mr. Yanamoto, obviously!

SW: Other than cartels and street gangs, I've heard that, according to the head of the FBI, so-called "white supremacist" are the biggest threat to democracy in this country. Shouldn't we be talking about those guys too?

Rx: See-Saw, excuse me, Mr. Iravani, you really like to veer off onto the tangential.

PM: Yoshi, you've laid out the landscape well regarding the causes and predicament many minority groups are experiencing and how problematic it is to ameliorate the circumstances. I would like to comment on the topic Shahzad introduced. Yes, Mr. Christopher Wray is the director of the FBI now, and yes, he did state, before a congressional committee, that white supremacy is the biggest domestic terror threat. There are groups like the Ku Klux Klan and Nazis, of course, but also, right-wing militias can fall under the general heading of white nationalists. They'd like to keep America all white and non-Jewish and gun-toting.

ET: Yoshi and Shahzad, you two gentlemen continue to ask some very pertinent questions regarding our look at, and possible solutions to, the gun violence issues in our land. With regard to the mental state of many young men brought up in poverty-stricken areas, where unhealthy neighborhoods encompass their daily lives, you have stated the objective situation about these young men. However, looking deeper into their family life, upbringing, and mental perspective on a subjective basis is also very valuable. Unfortunately, some of these young men had moms who were drug-addicted or parents who were addicted while raising them. At an early age, many in bad neighborhoods are introduced to drugs and criminal activities, or, in many cases, are intimidated and coerced into going along with neighborhood gangs.

KO: I'd like to offer some information about the militias that Mark mentioned. I've read a survey that the Anti-Defamation League published years ago regarding these groups. One of the significant findings is that many, thousands, believe the U.S. government is their enemy because the government is getting bigger, becoming more authoritarian and planning warfare against the citizens of the country, including coming for their guns. They believe they have to be prepared to fight.

Rx: You guys just want to find boogeymen under every rock. Most of the men in these militias are good, patriotic citizens who believe they have a personal responsibility to protect our democracy from a takeover by a president and government wanting to take their freedom to keep and bear arms away from them. They are good servants, not a threat the government as long as the government doesn't try to take away our God-given rights stated in the Second Amendment.

KO: There's nothing in the Second Amendment that specifies that the right to keep and bear arms is a "God given right."

Rx: Well, KO, it mentions the need for a "well-regulated militia."

KO: As I've pointed out in the history lesson, following the War of 1812, we didn't need a well-regulated militia to defend our country because we had a well-regulated, substantial standing army at that time and ever since.

Rx: You don't get it, KO. These paramilitary groups are not out to defend our country from external enemies, they're protecting us from internal enemies, the feds…

PM: You actually believe you need a paramilitary organization to protect you from whom? Our army, navy, marines? No, they're not charged with coming after you. The National Guard? No, they're not coming after you. Federal marshals, the ATF, the FBI? You're living in a fantasy world, not the real world. There are too many people, including police officers, veterans, hunters, and many others, including me, who would join militia groups to defend their Second Amendment rights if someone tried to forcibly take guns away. With that, I need to sign off. Bye.

SW: Aren't the white nationalist groups like the Proud Boys and the Oath Keepers part of the militia groups you're talking about? Weren't members in those groups involved in the January 6th, 2021, attack on the Capitol Building? Did they think the congressional people were going to take away their guns?

Rx: No, See-Saw, those patriotic guys were defending democracy. They believed the 2020 election was stolen from their candidate, and they were there to stop it from being finalized. They were defending freedom, and freedom isn't free.

ET: Gentlemen, we can argue about the militias until the cows come home. As far as I know, they'll not involved in a lot of homicides, just violence in the streets with the opposition. Why not talk about ongoing, daily occurrences of homicides? I'm talking about domestic violence. If a gun is in the home, the risk of a homicide increases by up to 500 percent according to studies. Roughly two women a day are killed by their spouse, boyfriend or relative. Sometimes, a man is murdered. We should be focusing on the causes and preventative measures if we seriously wish to do something about gun violence in our country.

Rx: Okay, let's move on to another vicious group of murderers in our country: men.

YY: Is it a problem with fear, or is it hate, or do the shooters get so angry they just get a gun and kill?

KO: Thanks Emily for broaching the domestic violence problem. It has been around a long time and many, many thousands of people have been murdered by a so-called "intimate partner." I'm sorry, but I can't stay and discuss it now. One of my grandsons has a ball game I'm supposed to be at. Take care everyone.

ET: Clyde, this isn't an issue to make fun of. If your daughter or granddaughter was in a relationship with a man who had a serious problem controlling his anger and he had a gun in the house, would you be a little bit concerned for her safety?

SW: Like Mark and Roberto, I now have something else to tend to. However, Emily I sure want to know more about this domestic violence issue. Good evening all.

ET: Yoshi, a shooting can be predicated on any one of the emotions you mentioned.

Rx: ET, I mean Mrs. Thurmond, I won't bother you anymore today. One of my sons, by the way, is a hunter and has a number of rifles stored in a very secure vault in his home. And his wife likes it when he "brings home the bacon" after hunting a few days. She has never displayed any concern to me about guns in the home.

YY: Emily, I guess we need to say goodbye too. It's ironic that you and I are still in the room. You're on the eastern side of the country, and I am on the western side.

CHAPTER SEVEN

Shahzad spent most of this Thursday morning on his computer and smartphone searching for as much information as he could find regarding domestic violence issues in the United States, and in particular how much of it occurred within the Muslim community. Within the Muslim community generally, he knew that women had learned to conceal abuse by their husbands, but divorce was an option for them. As a result, he couldn't find a lot of data. It was generally assumed that the occurrences were probably equal to those within the U.S. population overall. At 3:00 p.m., Central Standard Time, he put his laptop on a small table resting on the arms of his most comfortable recliner and entered his favorite Zoom room.

KO: Yeah, Yoshi, I'm letting it grow a bit longer. I guess I'm a bit lazy and cautious about going to the barbershop. A lot of guys here resist wearing masks.

ET: I wish I just had a problem with long hair. Mine is more a problem with graying and thinning.

KO: Talking about graying, Shahzad, your beard seems to have resisted graying since we have been in the room sharing our thoughts and ideas over the years.

YY: My bigger concern is my loss in height. I used to be 5'9", now I'm not quite 5'8".

ET: That common to almost all mature folks like us. Women tend to lose even more inches than men.

Rx: What's happening to our room? Has it been reduced to complaining about our biological deterioration with aging? I'm still over six feet and proud of it.

PM: Hi everyone. I think we'd better return to our focus on gun violence before Clyde continues giving us measurements on different parts of his anatomy.

Rx: Ha, Ha, PM. I can see that you've lost most of your hair. Was that due to all those frightful experiences you had as a rookie patrolman?

SW: I spent most of my morning hours looking into the domestic violence issue regarding Muslim communities in the U.S. I couldn't find much data about homicides within Muslim families. It's generally assumed that statistics are about the same as those for the general population of the U.S. I've heard of some. There's a lot more data about homicides and hate crimes against Muslims in this country.

Rx: Oh boy, now we're going to be condemning people of faith for gun violence in this great country of ours. It's starting out with Muslims by a Muslim, but I bet it going to proceed to Christians and even Lutherans. That's where I may get defensive.

KO: Yes, Clyde, you're correct in thinking that there are, unfortunately Christians who believe the federal government is their enemy. Have you heard of the Christian Identity group? They believe God has ordained them to defend the white race.

YY: Are they armed like other militias?

Rx: I'm sure you know, SW, about Sharia law and how barbaric it is toward women of the Muslim faith. How can you defend it?

SW: Well, Clyde, here in the U.S., laws have been passed to reduce the harmful effects that some Muslim men impose on their wives by interpreting it the way they do. However, there are Muslim activist women in some majority Muslim countries who are actually using Sharia to enhance their rights. Sharia can be interpreted in different ways. I'm not an expert, but that's what I've read over the years.

KO: Actually, I would like to focus on a different element of gun violence that is much more prevalent and results in more deaths by guns than militias or right-wing Christian conservative groups. Mark, you may not like this aspect of the total picture of gun violence in our country, but it's significant, and that is the number of people killed by police shootings in the U.S., each year. I know you don't trust statistics, Clyde; however, I think the rest of us appreciate them somewhat. The combined populations of England, Wales, Japan, and Germany are about 280 million people. That's about four-fifths of the population of the U.S. at about 330 million. The U.S. has over 1,000 people killed by police shooting them on average every year. Those four countries combined have, on average, only 16 people killed by police shootings every year. They had the same ratio as we do, they would have 800 or more people per year killed by police shootings. What does this say about our country?

ET: Those are horrible numbers! I've also known for some time that a disproportionate number of Black people are among those killed by police shootings here in our country. What a shame and an embarrassment for our country.

Rx: Those statistics, if credible, are easy to challenge. We have far more crime in this country and more people challenging police authority.

PM: No, Roberto, I'm not offended by your remarks. We have about 18,000 law enforcement agencies, police and sheriffs' departments, highway patrol, state police, and others, that have authority to use guns in their duties. There are about 700,000 officers employed in all those agencies. We know there are bad apples, racists, even bands of tattooed officers symbolizing their mutual biases or whatever. . . .

YY: And another aspect of your narrative, Roberto, is that most police in those other countries don't guns on the streets or in their cars, so shooting a suspect Isn't a readily available option.

Rx: Yeah, Yoshi, but most of the scum those officers in other countries have to deal with aren't toting guns.

PM: You're right, doctor, that's our whole point: less guns, less shootings and killings.

ET: Gentlemen, if I may, I'd like to go off on a tangent and return to the victims arena again. It seems to me that folks who want to apply the Second Amendment so that millions of Americans can possess a gun really don't know, unless it happened to a family member, relative, friend, colleague or neighbor, just how absolutely terrible it is for the victim's family, especially a loving mother. I know I covered this topic regarding the VT shooting, but I'd like to expose you guys to another shooting incident. May I?

Rx: ET, you want to expose us to another tearjerker? We know what death is all about.

PM I think I have a good feel for the gravity of suffering a family or friend endures, Emily, but we all have to learn about the degree of hurt a shooting brings on. We need those who support gun ownership to be exposed to the suffering more.

SW: Emily, I'm ready to listen and cry.

KO: Please, Emily, tell us about the incident to which you are referring.

ET: This incident happened in the city in which Mark worked as a police officer: Pasadena, California. A thirteen-year-old boy was playing a video game in his bedroom in the early evening. A bullet, perhaps stray as police conjectured, came through a window and hit him. He died in his mother's arms. I would like for you gentlemen to imagine all that mother had gone through with her son before that moment. Thirteen years and some months before, she realized or was told she was pregnant. She probably was excited, but maybe her husband wasn't as excited because there would be another mouth to feed, a child to clothe, and less sex. She had to pay attention to what her obstetrician told her about prenatal care. At some point, she would have to get clothes that fit, experience morning sickness, back pain, and be more careful physically, and, of course, deal with gain. And, of course, she had to go through this for a long nine months until birth, but during that time she would feel an emerging intimate attachment with that growing fetus within her womb.

YY: I guess I'd forgotten what my wife had to deal with each of our two children.

Rx: I hope you didn't hear me snoring. Actually, I served lots of women who benefited from meds prescribed by their OB-doc.

KO: Please continue, Emily.

ET: Then comes the most challenging stage: giving birth, either through the birth canal or by C-section. Most women who have given birth the natural way say they went through the most excruciating pain they ever experienced. From the moment the baby is born, the mother and dad have the gigantic responsibility to care for a completely helpless infant. The mother may breastfeed her baby. If not, she needs to provide formula for the baby to be nursed with. Someone has to watch and care for the infant for months until it is a toddler. At that phase, the child has a lot of energy to burn, so he or she can get into many things, even climb stairs. Parents need to start teaching the toddler, then the child, to do all sorts of things, including language, obedience, manners, and even activities like swimming. Then there's school, vaccinations, more clothes, learning how to take care of oneself, like brushing teeth and tying shoelaces and even activities like playdates and relationships. The mom can become completely exhausted trying to carry out all her perceived responsibilities. Also, keep in mind that many moms have more than one child to raise, as well as grocery shopping, cooking, cleaning the house, etc.

Rx: Please, Emily, on that note, I think most of us guys know what's involved because we've participated in raising the kids. I know sports and activities like hiking, sailing, and camping come into play, where the dad is very active.

PM: Okay, Clyde, you've made your point. What's the bottom line you wish for us "gentlemen" to perceive and understand, Emily?

ET: Thanks, Mark, and Clyde, you're right. However, there are lots of single moms raising kids. What I was attempting to impart is that the mother of that thirteen-year-old boy who was murdered had invested so much of her life, physically, emotionally, financially, and in time, into his life. To have it all go away in such a horrific way can be totally devastating to her. The loss will be with her for the rest of her life. Do you feel her pain and grief? Would you want your mother, wife, sister, or any woman you know to go through such an ordeal?

SW: Thank you, Emily. You have enlightened me substantially about what is lost when a child is lost in any way, but even more so in such a terrible way, and the loss the parents, especially the mother, have to deal with.

YY: Why are there some women who believe in allowing men to own guns when it's men who are involved in domestic abuse killings of their wives or girlfriends; men who carry out mass shootings; men (and boys) who are in gangs that kill each other in so many big cities; men who use guns to commit crimes like robberies; men in militias that threaten our government; and men who kill police officers? It seems to me that any woman who has gone through the motherhood experience you described so passionately, Emily, wouldn't want any guns anywhere.

ET: Let's call it a day, okay? Thanks for putting up with my lecturing. Good evening.

Rx: I'll second that. Don't forget to take your meds.

CHAPTER EIGHT

Mark spent some of his time between Zoom sessions rereading and checking the latest updates on the status of the situation with the Pasadena PD and the murder of the thirteen-year-old boy in that city. While relaxing in his recliner, he went into his memory and retrieved some similar incidents he had encountered as an officer. The rehashing of those violent events in his mind was painful.

SW:　Yes, I am trying to put together a draft proposal for remodeling a senior center in my community.

YY:　That's very nice of you to think of sharing your expertise and ideas and serving your community. Do you use that facility for any activities?

KO:　Good afternoon buddies. I hope I'm not interrupting something important.

SW:　No, Roberto, I was telling Yoshi about a project I'm dealing with. What's new with you?

PM:　Hi guys. In our session today, I'd like to provide an update on the killing of that 13 year old boy who was shot in his bedroom.

SW:　Hi Mark, what can you tell us about that terrible killing?

ET:　Good afternoon, gentlemen. Yes, Mark, I'm curious about the status of the police investigation. I know the family and friends are suffering a lot.

Rx: PM, before you give your police report in minute detail, I'd like to say to SW that the community room in my city's community center has been remodeled and I'm not entirely pleased with the results. The architects should have gotten some input from the users of the old facility.

PM: A number of things have happened since the violent killing took place. One was a community candlelight vigil with speakers including the mayor who said officials in the city have asked the police department to step up its enforcement and increase the number of officers on the streets. Contrary to that a prominent Latino activist said "We don't want to see SWAT teams coming into our neighborhoods" and "going after young men and young women of color. A city councilman stated that the city isn't prepared to police our way out of all the shootings and killings in the city. Then the city government and the LA County supervisors put up a $30,000 reward fund for assistance in apprehending the killer. The PD did offer the fact that it had taken 288 guns off the street last year, but there was no mention of the bigger picture of changing laws restricting gun ownership in any way.

KO: Yes, Mark, that's what is looming over the violence in America. The country just hasn't focused on the most obvious problem. It's almost beyond our capability to see what's right in front of our eyes. It's not just how many guns we have in the US, it's who owns them. Canada has about the same populations and number of gun owners as California, however, Canada had about 743 gun-related homicides in 2020, whereas California had about 2,161, almost three times as many.

YY: Does Canada have stricter gun ownership laws? We know it doesn't have a second amendment in its constitution. Or is it the demographic make up that so different?

Rx: No, YY, I mean Yoshi, it's our geographic location as mentioned previously. We have a southern border with Mexico, the drug cartel capital of the world. Illegal drug trafficking is out of control!

SW: So, Clyde, what are you suggesting, close the border completely? You do know Mexico is one of our largest trading partners. How are our imports and exports supposed to navigate a closed border?

ET: Gentlemen, it's not just one aspect of our culture, laws, geography, drug use, etc. It's the mindset of too many Americans along with our mental health system and other detrimental aspects of our society.

KO: Emily, that mindset you referred to has been dominant when it comes to wars. Our country has been involved in more wars over the past one hundred years than any other nation. We spend far more dollars on our military than any other country. Guns and other weapons of war are so prevalent among Americans.

RX: There you go again, KO, with your lambasting of our superior country. You don't mention why we have been involved in so many wars. Should we not have taken on the Germans for sinking so many of our ships in World War I, or the Japanese for attacking Pearl Harbor, or the communists who tried and succeeded in taking over South Vietnam? Let's have some transparency when spinning the facts.

ET: Since I've been in this room with you gentlemen, we have elucidated the gun violence problem in our country pretty well with facts, figures, personal narratives, and so on. Do we need to reveal more information, or are we going to seek out and share possible ideas and solutions to this extremely terrible and tragic problem our country faces every single day? Is this a project you intelligent, well-educated gentlemen wish to commit yourselves to? If so, I am willing to work with all of you to the best of my ability and energy. Otherwise, I don't know how much longer I will feel good about continuing to participate in the room. I hope I'm not coming off as controlling, condescending, or belligerent. I like you guys, but I want to get something done.

ET: Continuing to participate in the room, I hope I'm not coming off as controlling, condescending, or belligerent. I like you guys, but I want to get something done.

Rx: Emily, maybe you are an ET, since you believe this so-called problem you guys are fussing over is solvable. You guys have come up with all kinds of facts and figures and sad stories regarding gun homicides in the USA, but let me enlighten you a little. The USA has the third-largest population on the planet. China controls its people with an iron fist, so people can't own guns. If that country has homicides, do you think it would release facts and data to the world? India, the next country with a huge population, has mostly poor people who can't afford guns. So that leaves the USA with lots of people who can afford guns and the freedom to own them. Would you rather we be in India or China? Also, friends, our country has the greatest diversity of people because almost everyone wants to immigrate here because of our freedoms and economic and educational opportunities. Because we have so much money floating around, there's too much illegal drug use and too many gangs, which drive up the numbers of homicides significantly. The solution, Emily, is to stop the Mexican cartels from bringing those damn drugs into our country and jail those who are peddling them on our streets. Let's build the wall all across our southern border. Problem solved!!!

PM: As was mentioned previously, Clyde, Mexico is one of our greatest trading partners. Over a million commercial trucks enter the U.S. over our southern border every year. That's 3,000 trucks per day with lots of containers, boxes, etc. No wall is going to prevent them from coming into the U.S.

SW: Here's a little bit of info about India I just googled. There are lots of guns in India. There are over 61 million illegal firearms in India. That country has the fifth-highest number of firearm-related deaths. Where our country had over 37,000 such deaths, India had about 14,000 in 2019. But the population, as you probably know, is about four times that of the U.S. If India's gun-related deaths were on par with ours, that 14,000 figure would be more like 56,000. So, Clyde, I think you should do some checking before you make the assertions you do.

KO: I don't know if you folks are aware of what former Supreme Court Justice Stevens suggested as a change to the Second Amendment that, according to his thinking and reasoning, could amend the Second Amendment and substantially reduce gun violence in this country. His additional five words are when serving in the militia. So if the founders had placed those five qualifying words in the Second Amendment, only people who were serving in the militia could keep and bear arms. The whole idea back then was to have people possess guns in order to protect the country. As I've pointed out, once we had organized a standing army to defend our country, the ordinary citizen was no longer needed to defend it.

Rx: KO, I mean, Professor Roberto, I know you wish to come across as eloquent and elucidating to us students in your classroom; however, what you have proffered doesn't in any way pertain to our present era and predicament. You're not suggesting, are you, that all the millions of gun owners give up their guns because the founders left out five words in the Second Amendment?

YY: Here's an idea I haven't heard of before that the city of San Jose, California, has come up with. The city council recently passed a new ordinance that requires most gun owners in that city to buy liability insurance on their guns so that if someone gets shot or killed accidentally, or if there is damage done, the insurance will have to cover the costs.

Rx: Is this going to be a serious search for something that actually can reduce gun violence in this country, or are you guys just going to throw out irrelevant, cockamamie nonsense?

ET: Yoshi, I read an article about that ordinance. The thing I like about it is that it requires gun owners to pay an annual fee to register their guns. The money will help provide more mental health assistance and suicide prevention, as well as gun safety programs. All cities should do something like that.

Rx: I just can't believe you guys!!! You think law-abiding citizens should have to register the guns that help protect their families from intruders and murderers? This violation of our Second Amendment rights won't hold up in court, so it's just a waste of time to talk incessantly about it now.

SW: Mark, are you still with us? I'd like to know what your thoughts are regarding reducing gun violence in our country.

PM: Thanks, Shahzad. Unfortunately, Clyde could be correct regarding the courts, especially the Supreme Court, due to its current justices. I think deterrence of trafficking in illegal guns should be an area of possible enhancement. The ATF and state agencies dealing with illegal gun sales should be allocated more funds.

KO: Your remarks are all illuminating, Mark, Emily, and Yoshi, and we should not neglect taking Clyde's thoughts into the mix. There are many avenues we can look at as possible sources of solutions. I'll do some research on what has already been tried but was unsuccessful, and the reasons for the lack of success. However, for now, I need to depart. Take care.

ET: Oh my, I must depart too. Have a great evening, everyone!

Rx: Before you proceed, Ms. or is it Mrs.Thurman, I hope you aren't trying to take us into some kind of fairy-tale land. My time is too valuable for that kind of nonsense.

ET: No, Clyde, I'm not. It's Ms., by the way. The article is about what most gun owners traditionally believe about owning and having a gun's protection in their home. In a survey, 67 percent of gun purchasers believe having a gun is good for self-protection. Is that why you have guns in your home?

Rx: Of course! I'm not a hunter, and I don't go to a shooting range for target practice. Guns are good protection and make folks feel safe.

PM: I still own my service pistol from nearly twenty years ago. I keep it in my fireproof filing cabinet drawer that is locked. It would take me several minutes to get it if an intruder got into my home at night.

ET: Mark, I'm sure you are very proficient using it if needed. Do any of you gentlemen own a handgun or rifle?

SW: Not me.

YY: Ditto that!

KO: I used to own a BB gun, and I may still have it somewhere in my home, but I sure don't have it for self-protection.

Rx: You guys are risking your lives and the lives of your family members by not having a firearm for protection in today's United States.

KO: We're all about the same age, within a few years. I've never had to confront an intruder in my home or yard during my eighty-plus years of life.

SW: Me neither.

YY: I'll ditto that.

ET: I've never owned a gun, and I've never needed one to protect myself. In fact, the writer of this article states statistics that reveal that having a gun in the home makes it nine times more likely that you or a family member will be injured or killed with it than protected by one. The stakes are pretty grim.

Rx: Madam, you're distorting reality somewhat. Many people who die by gunshot with their own firearm in their home commit suicide, thousands of them every year. Subtract their numbers and you won't have a ninefold figure. Let's be honest when using statistics, PLEASE!

PM: Speaking as a former police officer, Clyde, I can tell you this: most home intruders are burglars. They don't want you to be home. They want to get in, get your good stuff, and leave without any confrontation. They may not even be armed. There are many, up to about 2.5 million a year in the U.S.

YY: That figure is very hard to imagine. That's almost 7,000 home invasions per day, or 680 per hour. About how many homeowners with guns do confront home invaders, and what are the results, generally? Obviously, most of those burglars, home intruders don't get shot.

Rx: There you guys go again, careening out of control with your statistics and numbers. I thought we'd agreed with ET to try coming up with some solutions to your gun violence problem.

KO: According to what I can find, there are more like 1.3 million a year, Mark. However, there are only about 100 homicides involving intruders in homes. I haven't been able to find info about the ratio of homeowners with guns versus the intruder who was shot. Probably the number is greater when those wounded are included. All the info I can find indicates it's more dangerous to have a gun in your home than not having one, as Emily stated earlier.

SW: Lots of calculations, Yoshi. Here's one for you: those burglars don't get shot. They steal about 170,000 guns from those law-abiding homeowners who have a gun in their homes for self-protection. How ironic is that?

YY: And what's the result of those burglaries? More criminals have guns they probably could not buy legally. They don't have to have a background check to see if they are allowed to buy a gun. They probably sell those guns to gang members so they can buy drugs to feed their addictions.

PM: You guys sound like police officers or people who have studied what crime is all about in this country. Congratulations.

SW: We know all of this now because we've been in this room with you, Roberto and …

RX: I'm not sorry to intrude on your touting parade. The gun owners whose homes are burglarized also lose lots of jewelry, artwork, cash, electronic devices, etc. The scum grab anything that they can sell easily. The homeowner will usually have homeowners insurance and can buy a replacement weapon. Should homeowners not have iPads in their homes because burglars will steal them? Even what Yakety Yak, I mean Yoshi is posturing with his big numbers, in a ratio of guns owned in this country to those stolen in burglaries, is almost noncomparative.

CHAPTER NINE

It was almost noon when Clyde left the pharmacy he used to own and operate. He liked to check out the place to see what was new and always hoped the new owner, after the nearly nine years since he sold it, was still doing okay because he and his wife were carrying a hefty loan on the building and business. He picked up some masks that his wife had requested. He didn't use them unless forced to. Soon it would be time, after eating lunch and making some calls, to go online to keep his chatroom liberals in line.

KO: The Omicron virus is still causing havoc in many of the hospitals in my state. Those who would prefer to die of it rather than succumb to getting vaccinated are doing just that—dying. That's got to be considered a form of suicide, it seems to me, especially if those folks have underlying medical conditions or are obese or elderly.

PM: Yes, Roberto, it's a shame what some people are doing to themselves, their families, friends, or employers. I know a man in his early sixties who refused to obey medical recommendations given by top scientists and doctors to be vaccinated. He listened to all the wrong advice from the anti-vaxxer groups. He was obese and drank a lot. He died within a week or so after contracting the virus. He made his choice because he wanted to be free and not ordered to do something by the government.

Rx: Professor, you probably were comfortable ordering your students to read something, write a paper, or complete some other requirement in order to pass your class. But that's not how most independent adults want to be:

obedient to some government official, even if that official is the surgeon general. They like to think for themselves and decide what they wish to do. Yes, some do make the wrong choices, as we all do, regarding their health. They really resent being told what to do by scum they don't respect. Besides that, there's some pretty credible evidence that what we've been told by the CDC and other political officials is not always all the facts. Just listen to some opinions from opposing points of view; you might be surprised by some of the findings and facts that are very substantial and rooted in good research.

ET: I see you gentlemen are off on another tangent, one obviously very concerning for our times. However, if it's okay with you men, I'd like to speak about another aspect of an overall solution to reduce gun violence in the USA. I found a newspaper article online that caught my eye. The title is: "Don't Buy into the Myth of Owning a Gun for Self-Defense." Would that headline pique your interest, Clyde?

ET: I've been reading about a study that took place in my neck of the woods, so to speak—Atlanta, Georgia. This study looked at incidents over an eight-week period in 1994. The objective was to study the epidemiology of home invasion crimes and determine the frequency with which firearms are used to resist these crimes. One hundred ninety-eight cases were studied. The homeowner and invader were acquainted in one-third of the cases. In only thirty-two cases did the offender carry a firearm. In 42 percent of the cases, the invader fled without confronting the victim. In sixty-two break-ins, there was a confrontation with weapons. In forty of those, the homeowner was injured.

Conclusion: Victims who avoided confrontation were more likely to lose property but much less likely to be injured. "Although firearms are often kept in the home for protection, they are rarely used for this purpose." Is it worth the cost, risks, and the protection guns actually offer?

PM: I remember reading that study back then. That had an impact on my thinking and on what I advised friends to do. Thanks for relating that to us.

RX: More studies and figures, where's your proposed solution, counselor?

KO: Doctor, I assume you're going to accuse me of sounding professorial, but I must inform you that incorporated within the study Emily so correctly related are solutions to our gun violence problem. If 170,000 guns are stolen each year by burglars, the way to reduce the number of guns criminals have is to not have homeowners provide them. And since, as stated in the study, homeowners who do have a gun for self-protection are more likely to be injured than those who don't possess a gun, therefore part of the solution to reducing gun violence in our nation is for homeowners to accept the fact that guns don't protect them and to not supply criminals with guns via burglaries.

Rx: Before I check out of this room, KO, I just want to enlighten you a little. People buy guns for a variety of reasons, not just for self-protection. You must know, living in New Mexico, that lots of people like to go hunting with their guns. I don't, but I have friends who do. You must know that there are folks who like to practice shooting their guns, skeet and targets. For me, I like to collect rifles that appeal to my sense of uniqueness. Lots of people in rural areas can feel a bit isolated and live too far from police protection. So think demographics and multiple purposes for guns. I've had enough of your solutions for now. Don't get too sure of yourselves.

ET:	There's something to say about geography as well. Southern white men are more likely to own guns than northeastern white men. And with that bit of revelation, we do need to concentrate more on solutions. I also need to say bye for now. Hope to be with you next Tuesday.

CHAPTER TEN

After enjoying his a fabulous lunch with his buddies at one of his favorite sushi restaurants near the beach, overlooking the waves of the Pacific Ocean, Yoshi got into his Lexus to drive to his home in Irvine. He was excited about a news story he saw on his smartphone regarding a large settlement in a lawsuit against the Remington gun manufacturer.

PM: Perhaps Clyde has a point about white men buying guns for other reasons, but most women, no matter what their race, buy guns primarily for self-protection.

KO: I think surveys have supported that conclusion. There are lots of men in this area who like hunting. As Emily suggested, geography does play a role to some extent regarding gun ownership.

YY: Good afternoon, Mark and Roberto. Is there anyone else in the room now? I don't see anyone else.

ET: I'm here. I just left for a moment to get something to drink. Mark, I know your statement is accurate. I don't believe I've ever counseled a gun-owning woman who got pleasure from collecting guns or who went hunting for sport. They hope to protect themselves from an intruder who might try to rape them or hurt them or their children somehow.

Rx: I see all of you are already trying to subjugate my remarks about the variety of reasons why people own guns. You keep challenging the veracity of my knowledge.

YY: All of you probably have heard the news about the Sandy Hook parents winning a big lawsuit against the Remington gun manufacturer. Wasn't that a surprise? I don't recall hearing about another lawsuit decision like that.

ET: Are you suggesting, Clyde, that we shouldn't disclose facts that we know to be true because those facts might undermine the validity of one of your conclusions? That sounds like something Putin of Russia would support. Why would we even wish to participate in this room if we need to suppress our knowledge and feelings? That wouldn't be mentally healthy.

SW: Hi, everybody. Yeah, Yoshi, I heard about that case. That seventy-three-million-dollar settlement must really put a chill on all the gun manufacturers. Maybe that decision can be incorporated into our solution.

KO: I'm glad you brought up that settlement, Yoshi. It's almost unfathomable when considering the law that was passed years ago by Congress and signed by President Bush, which protects gun manufacturers from being held liable for harm done by their products. The only protection the American people got from the deal was a mandate that handguns had to have safety locks.

Rx: Common sense tells you that the manufacturers needed some cover of law. Otherwise, anyone shot could sue the manufacturer as well as the perpetrator of the shooting. No guns would be made if that were allowed.

SW: What, Roberto, is actually covered under that law?

YY: Are other industries protected from lawsuits like the gun manufacturers are? Like the auto industry? Drug companies? Knives? Fireworks?

KO: Even with the Protection of Lawful Commerce in Arms Act protecting them, gun manufacturers can still be sued like any consumer products manufacturer. They're not completely off the hook, as this settlement reveals. They are protected if a gun is stolen and the criminal shoots someone, if the police use a gun, or if a homeowner accidentally shoots a family member. Yoshi, vaccine manufacturers can be protected as well.

PM: Yes, Roberto, and they can be sued if the weapon is defective somehow. And in this Sandy Hook case, they marketed a very dangerous weapon while not following restrictions that gun dealers are supposed to adhere to.

Rx: Obviously, YY, pharmaceutical companies aren't protected; they're being sued every day. Even using FDA testing requirements and approval under the FDA's rigorous standards, and with many consumer warnings of side effects, pharmaceutical companies are very vulnerable.

ET: That's amazing, Clyde, considering the fact that the pharmaceutical and health industries have the most powerful lobby in Washington, D.C.

PM: I can tell you guys this: gun manufacturers aren't protected when it comes to police officers being injured by a defective gun. The manufacturers pay out big sums for those injuries. One officer had his semiautomatic handgun in a holster, and it fired, seriously injuring his leg.

SW: What was the situation like before this Protection Act was legislated?

KO: The manufacturers were being sued successfully. That's why they needed protection against lawsuits. Victims of gun violence prevailed in court.

SW: Who passed that law? That is, which political party was in control of Congress back then?

Rx: That's a political question, See-Saw. You must want to play the blame game. The law was needed. At some point, with all the lawsuits, the gun factories and gun dealers would have had to close their doors. Why don't you people want to discuss realistic solutions?

KO: Republicans, in both chambers, Shahzad.

PM: Some firearms issues present real conundrums and are much more complicated when trying to find a real solution that can be enforced. Fortunately, the courts have now opened a door with the Remington *v.* Sandy Hook parents case for some changes to come about. Ghost guns have presented bigger challenges for law enforcement to solve.

YY: Mark, what the heck are ghost guns anyway? I infer that they would be easy to conceal and hard to find.

Rx: Instead of going after guns, why don't we focus on mental health and drug addiction? As far as I'm concerned, those are the basis of domestic violence and inner-city gang violence.

PM: Try to explain your point of view to the families of those in Santa Monica, California, who were killed with a ghost gun a few years ago, Clyde. Yoshi, a ghost gun is sold in parts or components. They must be assembled by the buyer. The manufacturer doesn't have to place a serial number on these weapons. No background check is required to purchase one.

SW: How long have these weapons been around in the U.S.? Are there laws restricting them somehow?

PM: They've been around for almost thirty years, I think; however, they've only been popular in the past eight to ten years. Some states, I'd have to do some research, like California, have worked to put some controls on them. An owner of a ghost gun must acquire a serial number or some sort of identification from the Justice Department in California for the gun and place that on the gun itself.

ET: Clyde, in order to predict that a so-called "law-abiding citizen" will always be mentally healthy and not resort to violence would require far more resources than our mental health establishment could manage. Some people, looking at how they were raised, might be easy to identify, but why is it that boys raised in stable families turn out to be mass shooters? How could we predict that? If someone is suicidal, that could be a red flag. We'd have to be notified of every disgruntled employee to prevent mass shootings in workplaces. How are we going to prevent everybody who drinks too much alcohol from purchasing a gun? Mental illness comes in a lot of forms.

KO: Mark, it's good that California has established some significant gun controls. However, I read an article about some real complications relating to their enforcement. Apparently, due to multiple agencies and the courts being involved, some decisions and interpretations undermine the intent of the law. Emily just responded to the mental health issue that you raised, Clyde. Well, here is an example of the complications that are sometimes involved. A man who had been placed on a psychiatric list at one point was later able, months afterward, to obtain an AR-15. This man then assaulted a highway patrol officer after a drunk-driving accident and also assaulted an emergency room technician. His ex-girlfriend, the mother of the three girls who were killed, had obtained a restraining order so that he could only see his daughters with a chaperone present and only during scheduled visits at a church. During one of these visits, he shot his three children, the chaperone, and himself. During a court hearing, the ex-girlfriend told the court that she was unaware whether the killer, David Mora Rojas, owned a gun. The judge asked him if he did own a gun, and he answered "no," which was apparently good enough for the court. One of the problems was the lack of information sharing among various law enforcement agencies. Certainly, the court should have ordered a check of Mora Rojas's home to search for a gun. I hope I haven't put anyone to sleep with this monologue.

Rx: Yes, KO, you nearly put me to sleep. As usual, you guys leave out important info. Maybe the media you are reading or watching intends to brainwash you by not including pertinent facts. Because I heard about this shooting on my conservative talk shows and TV networks, I learned that this killer wasn't in the country legally. Besides that, when he was released from jail following his arrest for assaulting the CHP officer, ICE came looking for him. Because California is one of those God-awful states that gives sanctuary to illegal immigrant criminals, the police didn't turn him over for deportation. If he had been deported, those three innocent girls would be alive today.

PM: Clyde, I thought you would jump in with both feet. Yes, you are partially correct about Mora Rojas being in our country illegally, but you didn't say how he came in. He entered on a visa and overstayed his authorized time. What I also find interesting, Roberto, is that the AR-15 he used was found to be a ghost gun. Another aspect of this tragedy is that law enforcement has to deal with many thousands of criminals, and keeping track of them and searching for guns they may possess is an insurmountable task with the personnel most departments and agencies have.

Rx: Visa or no visa, that criminal should have been deported immediately!

KO: Clyde, do you really believe you get all the true facts from conservative media?

Rx: There you go again with your condescending, radical liberal, far left-wing socialist questioning of anything you haven't heard or don't believe in. You S.O.B.s think you know it all, but you've been brainwashed by liberal-progressive professors like you were and by left-wing, radical media. Get off your woke high horse and be open to the truth!

ET: Gentlemen, if we can't have a civilized discussion with all points of view heard, we will just be wasting our time in this room. I don't mind hearing all sides of an issue as long as real facts can be presented. If both of you are totally unwilling to accept any information from the other, how can we come to any possible solutions to the gun violence threat in our country? If we can't come to any agreement, how are we to think politicians can?

SW: If I can get a word in here, it does seem sensible to me that anyone in this country without the government's permission should have been deported if he or she assaulted a police officer, as well as a medical worker. ICE should have been able to do its job in this case. Sorry to disagree with you, Roberto.

KO: Mark, your point about that ghost gun is important. No serial number was found on it. For people like him, who would not be able to purchase a gun legally, ghost guns can be available. Enforceable laws need to be part of the solution to blocking an unauthorized person from acquiring a gun.

YY: I would like to say two things. Clyde, I am really concerned about you and others who get so very angry when something political is brought up. Maybe Roberto wasn't being very polite when he asked you that question, but he didn't call you any names or accuse you of anything. The second thing is something maybe we can look into. I remember that the mass shooter in Las Vegas had modified a gun so he could fire more shots rapidly. Isn't that in the same category as assembling a ghost gun?

PM: Yoshi, Paddock, the shooter, had converted his guns into automatic weapons with something called "bump stocks." They were legal to buy at the time. Congress couldn't get its act together, but the Justice Department did declare them illegal in 2018. They were classified as "machine guns." As you all know, it's very difficult to get much passed in Congress restricting guns in any way.

Rx: Yoshi, you may not respect yourself much and allow people to insult you, but a man of my prominence and intellect isn't going to let insults go by without challenging them. KO was being a smart-ass, and I'm not going to just ignore his insults. With that, I'm going to leave the room to watch my favorite commentators tell me the truth about the news of the day.

SW: If these gun modification devices are illegal now, how do criminals get them?

SW: Who passed that law? That is, which political party was in control of Congress back then?

Rx: That's a political question, See Saw. You must want to play the blame game. The law was needed. At some point, with all the lawsuits, the gun factories and gun dealers would have to close their doors. Why don't you people want to discuss realistic solutions?

KO: Republicans, in both chambers, Shahzad. If enough victims lawsuits prevailed, guns would be much more expensive. That would be good.

PM: Some firearms issues present real conundrums and are much more complicated when it comes to finding a real solution that can be enforced. Fortunately, the courts have now opened a door with the Remington *v.* Sandy Hook parents case for some changes to come about. Ghost guns have presented bigger challenges for law enforcement to solve.

YY: Mark, what the heck are ghost guns anyway? I infer that they would be easy to conceal and hard to find.

Rx: Instead of going after guns, why don't we focus on mental health and drug addiction? As far as I'm concerned, those are the basis of domestic violence and inner-city gang violence.

PM: Try to explain your point of view to the families of those in Santa Monica, CA, who were killed with a ghost gun a few years ago, Clyde. Yoshi, a ghost gun is sold in parts or components. They must be assembled by the buyer. The manufacturer doesn't have to place a serial number on these weapons, and no background check is required to purchase one.

SW: How long have these weapons been around in the U.S.? Are there laws restricting them somehow?

PM: They've been around for almost thirty years, I think. However, they've only been popular in the past eight to ten years. Some states—though I'd have to do some research—like California, have worked to put some controls on them. An owner of a ghost gun must acquire a serial number or some sort of identification from the California Department of Justice and place that on the gun itself. The weapon must be traceable.

ET: Clyde, predicting that a so-called "law-abiding citizen" will always be mentally healthy and never resort to violence would require far more resources than our mental health establishment could manage. Some people, looking at how they were raised, might be easy to identify, but why is it that those raised in stable families turn out to be mass shooters? How could we predict that? If someone is suicidal, that could be a red flag. Would we have to be notified of every disgruntled employee to prevent mass shootings in workplaces? How are we going to prevent everybody who drinks too much alcohol from purchasing a gun? Mental illness comes in many forms.

KO: Mark, it's good that California has established some significant gun controls. However, I read an article about some real complications relating to their enforcement. Apparently, due to multiple agencies and the courts being involved in enforcement, some decisions and interpretations undermine the intent of the law. Emily just responded to the mental health issue that you raised, Clyde. Well, here is an example of the complications that are sometimes involved. A man who had been placed on a psychiatric list at one point was later able, months afterward, to obtain an AR-15. This man then assaulted a highway patrol officer after a drunk-driving accident and also assaulted an emergency room technician. His ex-girlfriend, the mother of the three girls who were killed, had obtained a restraining order so that he could only see his daughters with a chaperone present and only during scheduled visits at a church. During one of these visits, he shot his three children, the chaperone, and himself. During a court hearing, the ex-girlfriend told the court that she was unaware whether the killer, David Mora Rojas, owned a gun. The judge asked him if he did own a gun, and he answered "no," and that was good enough for the court. One of the problems was the lack of information sharing among various law enforcement agencies. Certainly, the court should have ordered a check of Mora Rojas's home to search for a gun. I hope I haven't put anyone to sleep with this monologue.

Rx: Yes, KO, you nearly put me to sleep. As usual, you guys leave out important info. Maybe the media you are reading or watching intends to brainwash you by not including pertinent facts. Because I heard about this shooting on my conservative talk shows and TV networks, I learned that this killer wasn't in the country legally. Besides that, when he was released from jail following his arrest for assaulting the CHP officer, ICE came looking for him. Because California is one of those God-awful states that gives sanctuary to illegal immigrant criminals, the police didn't turn him over for deportation. If he had been deported, those three innocent girls would be alive.

PM: Clyde, I thought you would jump in with both feet. Yes, you are partially correct about Mora Rojas being in our country illegally, but you didn't say how he came in. He entered on a visa and overstayed his authorized time. What I also find interesting, Roberto, is that the AR-15 he used was found to be a ghost gun. Another aspect of this tragedy is that law enforcement has to deal with many thousands of criminals, and keeping track of them and searching for guns they may possess is an insurmountable task with the personnel most departments and agencies have.

RX: Visas or no visa, that criminal should have been deported immediately!

KO: Clyde, do you really believe you get all the true facts from conservative media?

RX: There you go again with your condescending, iniquitous, radical liberal, far left-wing, woke, socialist, communist questioning of anything you haven't heard or believe in. You F.O.B.s think you know it all, but you've been brainwashed by liberal-progressive professors like you were, and left-wing, radical media. Get off your woke high horse and be open to the truth!

ET: Gentlemen, if we can't have a civilized discussion with all points of view heard, we will just be wasting our time in this room. I don't mind hearing all sides of an issue as long as real facts can be presented. If both of you are totally unwilling to accept any information from the other, how can we come to any possible solutions to the gun violence threat in our country? If we can't come to any agreement, how are we to think politicians can?

SW: Roberto, it looks like you struck a nerve. If I can get a word in here, it does seem sensible to me that anyone in the country without the government's permission should have been deported if he or she assaulted a police officer, in addition to assaulting a medical worker. ICE should have been able to do its job in this case. Sorry to disagree with you, Roberto.

KO: Mark, your point about that ghost gun is important. No serial number was found on it. For people like him, who would not be able to purchase a gun legally, ghost guns can be available to them. Enforceable laws need to be part of the solution to blocking an unauthorized person from acquiring a gun.

YY: I would like to say two things. Clyde, I am really concerned about you and others who get so very angry when something political is brought up. Maybe Roberto wasn't being very polite when he asked you that question, but he didn't call you any names or accuse you of anything. The second thing is something maybe we can look into somewhat. I remember that the mass shooter in Las Vegas had modified a gun so he could fire more shots rapidly. Isn't that in the same category as assembling a ghost gun?

PM: Yoshi, Paddock, the shooter, had converted his guns into automatic weapons with something called "bump stocks." They were legal to buy then. Congress couldn't get its act together, but the Justice Department declared them illegal in 2018. They were declared "machine guns." As you all know, it's very difficult to get much passed in Congress restricting guns in any way.

Rx: Yoshi, you may not respect yourself much and allow people to insult you, but a man of my caliber and intellect isn't going to let insults go by without challenging them. KO was being a smart-ass, and I'm not going to just ignore his insults. With that, I'm going to leave the room to watch my favorite commentators tell me the truth about the news of the day.

SW: If these modification devices are illegal now, how do criminals get them?

PM: Shahzad, criminals can get them on the black market. A common device simply changes the trigger mechanism from single-shot to automatic firing.

VY: Emily, would you like to add any comments regarding my question about the anger issue? It seems there are too many people with very serious anger, specifically when it comes to politics. What's behind that? We all can have opinions and feelings regarding various controversial issues and aspects of our society and politics, but why become enraged over them?

ET: Yoshi, that is a key part of the solution to reducing gun violence, and I'll offer some of my perspective in our next chat room. In general, without my professional hat on, I believe the only way out of the terrible place our country and society are in is what humanity has done from its outset. That is, humanity has evolved. We humans are capable of growing and enhancing our abilities, not only from primitive existence to affluence, but also in how we see and deal with each other. Just look at the women's liberation movement from the 1960s to now. What a change in their position in our society. That's evolving, and that's what we must do regarding guns.

PM: Speaking of anger, Yoshi, we all can experience a little anger when driving and some inconsiderate driver cuts us off or goes through a red light. But there are people who are carrying guns in their cars whose anger becomes rage, and they seek revenge. That's called "road rage." This phenomenon has gotten worse since the pandemic hit our country.

KO: Here's some data about that, Mark. According to what I just found, 522 people were wounded or killed in the U.S. last year due to road rage. Obviously, lots of people don't just keep their guns at home.

SW: So, it's not just a matter of someone planning to shoot a lot of people, or a person mad at his employer or wife, trying to rob someone, gangs shooting each other, or someone breaking into someone's home; we also have ordinary people who can just get violent while driving. Is there a way to stop all of this from happening? I'm sorry, I can't wait for an answer. If anyone has one, I would like to hear it, but I've got to take care of a couple of things. Take care, all.

ET: We keep getting into more and more horrible, insufferable acts of violence. Digging humanity out of this dark, deep, horrific hole will take a lot of inspiration, vision, insight, and wisdom. Do we have it within ourselves to believe we can help calm the waters and create momentum in an evolutionary cultural track to alter our country's demented reality? I'll keep my mind and heart open for guidance, wisdom, and advice. Bye for now.

PM: I think that's it for today. Let's keep Emily's thoughts active in our minds.

KO: Your words are powerful and hopefully they'll inspire all of us to enroll in this great challenge.

CHAPTER ELEVEN

Shahzad spent his weekend reading and conversing with his wife about an article she showed him. She had been listening to the conversations he was having with his Zoom room political friends and was reminded of an article she had read that provoked some inspiring thoughts, which she decided to share with her husband. He was ready the following Tuesday to offer a follow-up to what Emily had said.

KO: Yes, Mark, road rage incidents are increasing rapidly in the U.S., partly due to the easy access of gun ownership. Someone is shot, either killed or injured, every 17 hours.

Rx: I see you guys have moved on from ghost guns. Now it's road rage. How fascinating!

PM: In the good old days, those of us who got ticked off at another driver would just resort to giving the "birdie" or yelling some four-letter words out the window at the other driver. Remember the good old days?

ET: I think I just honked. I still do. Good afternoon, everyone.

SW: Emily, I read a very interesting article, could be called, enlightening. That connected me to something you said last Thursday.

Rx: Oh, no! Just as I was practicing using my middle finger, See-Saw's going to take us on another tangent into the wilderness.

YY: Hi, everyone. I'd like to hear about your enlightening article, Shahzad.

ET: Me too. And how is it connected to something I said?

PM: Before we get into Shahzad's article, I'd like to add one other thing that used to be another road rage result, and a violent one, but without guns. That was fistfights. Sometimes people got seriously hurt in them. Six point eight percent of road rage incidents end in death, including car crashes. I had to deal with a few of those crashes as a rookie on the beat.

Rx: You're still a rookie, PM. Haha! How was that percentage determined?

KO: Class, let's get serious. Please give us what you have, Shahzad.

SW: I think I may have gotten some inspiration and guidance from a story my wife gave me to read. This article begins with these optimistic words, "I firmly believe everything humanity could ever need is already here, ready for us to use."

Rx: Let's not get into religion right now. We could debate it the rest of the day.

YY: Did the writer give any examples of what s/he was thinking about as evidence? That's definitely an optimistic view.

SW: The writer, a woman named Joanne McFadden yes, Clyde, a minister, also said in this article, "It seems as though Spirit has created a gargantuan puzzle for human beings to assemble."

Rx: How thought-provoking. Let me give you some quotes from the Holy Bible.

KO: Clyde, can't you have any respect for another person's interests?

SW: Yoshi, she goes on about vampire bats' saliva that is being researched for use as an anticoagulant to prevent blood clotting and strokes. It seems to me that if humans can put such a very unique piece of the puzzle into its correct place, maybe we can come up with a piece of the puzzle to do something that benefits humanity regarding gun violence.

ET: I'm with you, Shahzad. As I mentioned the other day, it's time that we focus on solving this, and we must believe—have faith—that there is a solution, even if it's just reducing the statistics somewhat involving gun violence in our nation.

KO: Okay, let's look at what we are up against insofar as causing the needle to move even a little. There's the Second Amendment of the Constitution. We have a Supreme Court that is there to protect that amendment and is made up primarily of justices who are very supportive of it. We also have the NRA and other gun rights organizations that fight tooth and nail to block or overturn laws that move the needle at all. Then we have a majority of people in the country, two-thirds, who support stricter gun control laws. Only 24 percent of a recent poll said the laws were the most important for the government to work on, and only 415

KO: Of Democrats. Politicians look at those numbers and the numbers for the other issues—the economy, immigration, inflation, and COVID-19 and they'll try to please their constituent base. Therefore, it's extremely hard to get a bipartisan bill of any nature passed. Then there are the gun manufacturers who want laws to protect them from liability, as we've seen in the recent Sandy Hook shooting case. There's also the problem that even if gun sales were terminated tomorrow, we have around 300 million guns already in existence in this country and many thousands of gangs and criminals ready to use the guns they have stolen or made, ghost guns. I could go on, but you can see some of the obstacles and hurdles we're facing in attempting to come up with anything impactful. It's discouraging and yet so vital. However, I'm willing to roll up my proverbial sleeves and put my thinking cap on to work with my partners to do what's within me to create change.

Rx: What a soliloquy!!! Why must you take up our time, Professor, regurgitating stuff we educated people already know? Are you imagining yourself back in the classroom?

VY: You sure know how to insult people, Clyde! I'm onboard, ready to tee off, with you, Emily, and Roberto. In some instances in my past, when a group of friends took on a project, we each took an element or section of it to do some research. That way, we covered a lot of areas of the project simultaneously. Perhaps we could separate this almost insurmountable project and each take an element to study and come up with some possible potentials for change.

PM: I can now understand more fully why you've experienced lots of success in your life, Yoshi. I think you've got a good, workable outline for a plan with a chance for some success. Like you, I'm onboard or perhaps, on duty.

ET: Thank you, Commander Jackson. What you said to Mr. Yanamoto was a wonderful example of politeness and cooperation. Doctor Graf, we get a lot more from other humans by giving them the acknowledgment and praise they deserve. Also, speaking of Roberto's summarizing of the aspects we have covered and will have to deal with, it was anodyne and comprehensive as far as I'm concerned, certainly not regurgitating anything.

Rx: I'm not in your office. I didn't come to you for a therapy session. To me, KO was biased and insulting with his kindergarten iteration.

SW: If I might, perhaps I could construct a list of a few sections or categories we could cover in our search for enlightenment. It seems to me that we need to deal with gun laws and courts, our social culture and politics, the enforcement system, gangs, the prison system, as well as illegal drug use and drug cartels, mental health, including its system of care, domestic violence, and education. The gun manufacturing industry also has to be dealt with. What did I miss?

PM: Good job, Shahzad! I think you've covered most of the essentials. As you would probably guess, I would be interested in tackling the law enforcement angle. There's a lot to improve on, encompassing all the aspects you've listed. I hope one of you takes on dumb laws like Stand Your Ground.

Rx: This will be an utter waste of my precious time. I'll see what I can offer on the drug issues. Drugs are obviously misused, and that misuse can bring on some dire consequences. PM, your feminine X-chromosome side is showing itself. What man would not stand his ground, with or without a gun, if confronted?

YY: Are you going to delve into the use of illegal drugs like cocaine and heroin?

Rx: I'm not going to delve into illegal drug trafficking and all the cartel crap, but I can educate you on how those illegal drugs screw up people's lives and health.

ET: I'm encouraged by your willingness to join in this effort, Clyde, even though you think it's a waste of your precious time. It could be the same for all of us. You probably had me in mind when you listed mental health, Shahzad, and of course you were right to think so, since that was my field of experience. The domestic violence aspect is a monumental part of gun violence and definitely requires scrutiny and intensive work to mitigate it in any way possible.

PM: Clyde, we are focusing on reducing homicides, not increasing them. With the Stand Your Ground laws in many states, thirty or more people are killed every month in the U.S. due to someone standing their ground with a firearm.

Rx: Patrolman, that's an insignificant number in the total number of homicides in our country, and probably most of those shot were the bad guys.

YY: That's 30 a month, or 360 a year. What Mark is talking about is much more than all the homicides in Japan every year. That's not insignificant!

KO: According to a RAND study regarding Stand Your Ground incidents, the homicide number Mark mentioned will continue to increase. Other factors to be considered are the lack of de-escalation training given to those who carry guns, concealed or open carry, and even more impactful is the inequality in court cases justifying the use of Stand Your Ground (SYG) homicide. It is ruled justified 281 percent more often in SYG cases when the shooter is white and the person shot is Black than if both parties are white.

PM: Roberto, since you mentioned Blacks being shot, what do you think about this ironic twist? An appellate court struck down a California law preventing 18- to 20-year-olds from purchasing an AR-15 and other guns, and it wasn't long after that decision came down that an 18-year-old white kid was able to purchase an AR-15 in Pennsylvania, modify it in order to use a bigger magazine, and then go into a supermarket and kill ten Black people in Buffalo, New York. That's a hate crime, and it is a significant number.

SW: One of the components of our solution could be what to do with all the 300 million-plus weapons people already have. Can we possibly reduce the numbers sold in the future?

PM: Good question, Shahzad. If we were able to successfully block all future gun sales, gun violence could continue to be awful. So, what action could the country take to reduce that staggering number of weapons? For a long time, the NRA and other gun organizations propagandized that the left wants to take all our guns away, so there would be a huge amount of resistance.

KO: Shahzad, you design plans. Could you work on designing a plan for how our country could reduce the number of guns in the hands of fellow Americans over the next 25 years, and what would we do with them once we have them?

YY: Following up on that thought a little, what do you think about me looking into all the countries that have laws limiting or prohibiting gun sales and what they did with any guns confiscated? Are their laws working successfully?

Rx: I'm trying to restrain myself from reacting to your childish notions. Even in twenty-five or fifty years, you left-wing radicals won't be taking anyone's guns from them without a fight. They'll die with their guns in their hands.

SW: If you are spot-on, as they say, Doctor, the only effect we could have on the number of guns in this country is the possibility of slowing down and perhaps terminating the sale of some guns like the AR-15. Should we just direct our attention to those possibilities? Or possibly a great buy-back deal?

PM: Yoshi, I like your idea about researching what other countries have done about gun sales restrictions or even whether any of them confiscated guns.

ET: Mark, the young man, Payton Gendron, underwent psychiatric evaluation for telling people at school that he would murder people and commit suicide after graduating from high school. He later claimed he was joking. He was released after a day and a half of treatment and not tracked on social media. Then, when he turned 18, he bought the AR-15 in another state and modified it to use a larger magazine. He used it to kill ten people and wound three in that Tops grocery store mass shooting. We obviously need a lot of government involvement when it comes to potential killers with mental illnesses.

SW: Emily, you've brought up a very important and obvious area that we need to explore in depth in order to do something about gun violence, including the effects and influence social media has on young men. That kid had learned about white supremacy on social media platforms. Who wants to tackle the tech problems? Or is it a social culture problem?

Rx: Yes, let's focus on the snafus those bizarre freaks Bill Gates, that left-wing radical con man Mark Zuckerberg, and that

Twitter idiot Jack Dorsey have brought on our country. A lot of craziness has befallen us because of their social media crap.

KO: Shahzad, I agree with you that social media should be an element of the solution to gun safety. The New Zealanders recognized it was an issue for them following a mass shooting in their country. Their prime minister, Jacinda Ardern, worked to get legislation passed to deal with extremism on social media and to pass gun safety laws. It's working there.

ET: Doctor Graf, your use of hyperbolic adjectives for the men you were referring to doesn't get us an inch closer to a solution. We need to try to be inclusive and solicit cooperation from all sides of the fragments of our gun violence and safety solution.

YY: Shahzad, I can include in my international research what other countries are doing to put some brakes on extremism and subsequent gun violence on their social media platforms.

KO: Another aspect, and a major one, is the structure of our legislative system. We don't have a majority-rule system of democracy due to what the Founding Fathers in the most populated states had to do: compromise, in order to bring the least populated states around to support the creation of our country. James Madison, the guy who got the Second Amendment into the Bill of Rights, also proposed a second chamber in the national legislature. So, Article I of the Constitution allows for a bicameral system with two senators from each state, thus giving Wyoming, the least populated state, equal power in the Senate as California, the most populated state. That took away majority rule in the U.S.A. I'll be willing to insert what has happened to gun safety legislation in Congress because of the compromise the Founding Fathers made.

Rx:　There you go again, in your delusional perspective, attacking the greatest democracy mankind has ever created. KO, you need to show gratitude that your parents migrated to this country. What is your native country, Peru, doing with democracy? I suppose at some point in the future, in our considerations, you'll propose what that demented John Paul Stevens suggested a few years ago: repeal the Second Amendment and take away people's rights.

YY:　Hey, wow! That's what should happen! No more homicides! We could just go for the jugular and take away everyone's idiotic right to own a gun and carry it around in public.

Rx:　YY, being of Japanese descent, you probably aren't aware of the last time an amendment was repealed in this country; otherwise, you wouldn't have shown such a low level of knowledge of the history of this great nation. People's rights to consume alcohol were taken away about a hundred years ago, and years later another amendment was passed to overturn that first takeover of constitutional rights.

VY:　Is there a right in the Constitution for us to consume alcohol or own a house like the right to own a gun?

KO:　No, Yoshi, there isn't. The chapter in our history Clyde is talking about happened when the Eighteenth Amendment was passed due to long-term efforts by people in something called the temperance movement, who gained a lot of political clout over the years. It was passed by Congress and ratified by 46 states in 1917. Then, in 1933, Congress and 37 states passed the Twenty-first

Amendment, which repealed the Eighteenth Amendment and gave states control over laws regarding alcohol. What Clyde is attempting to tell us is that if, by some miracle, the Second Amendment were repealed by a Twenty-eighth or later amendment, it would just be a matter of years before it, too, would be repealed.

PM: With the prohibition of alcohol, crime spiked with bootlegging and mobster gangs who sold and controlled illegal alcohol. Too many Americans wanted to consume alcohol. A similar action has been taking place in many states regarding cannabis now. With a prohibition of guns, as we previously discussed, there would still be over 300 million guns in the country, and if they weren't confiscated, homicides would continue to escalate for eons. They wouldn't be sold on an eBay kind of platform but on the black market, without any background checks, etc.

Rx: KO, you must be proud of your elite academic knowledge, but we really don't need your freshman-class interpretations.

YY: Thanks, Roberto, for elaborating in more detail what Clyde told us.

SW: Professor, maybe you can clear up something that caught my attention a day ago, but I didn't get my thoughts arranged well enough to ask you a good question. You have said that the gun culture in our country was originally brought from England and was kept in order to defend the new land and later, the country, from foreign invaders such as England, but then after the War of 1812–15, one of the reasons to maintain that culture was to be able to fight government oppression. Also, during all that time, people in some parts of the new land had to worry about Indians and/or pirates intruders entering their houses and stealing stuff and now guns are also used for protection from intruders. So, if we no longer have to worry about foreign invaders, Indians, and since, other than the Civil War, people haven't had to fight off government oppression in over 200 years, we are left with one reason to own a gun: home protection. And since you or Mark revealed we are safer without a gun in our home, it seems it would be very easy to convince most people that there's no need to own a gun. To me, it appears to be a concentric circle of a lot of arguments and justifications that contradict each other. Am I making any sense?

Rx: See-Saw, what you just took a lot of time trying to inquire about is antithetical to all the facts relating to crime in our country that have been regurgitated many times over the past several weeks in our Zoom sessions. You invoked KO's words as the only authority for the truth too much.

ET: Shahzad, are you basically reasoning that most of the rational reasons people have given for gun ownership have gone by the wayside? If statistically accurate, having a gun in your home is potentially more harmful than not having one.

Rx: An amendment was repealed in this country; otherwise, you wouldn't have shown your low level of knowledge of the history of this great nation. People's rights to consume alcohol were taken away about a hundred years ago, and years later another amendment was passed to restore that constitutional right.

YY: Is there a right in the Constitution for us to consume alcohol or heroin?

SW: Professor, maybe you can clear up something that caught my attention days ago, but I didn't get my thoughts arranged well enough to ask you a good question. You have said that the gun culture in our country was originally brought from England; then it was kept in order to defend the new land and later, the country, from foreign invaders such as England. But then, after the War of 1812–15, one of the reasons to maintain that culture was to be able to fight government oppression. Also, during all that time, people in some parts of the new land had to worry about Indians and/or pirate-type intruders entering their homes and stealing stuff, and now guns are also used just for protection from intruders. So, if we no longer have to worry about foreign

Rx: An amendment was repealed in this country; otherwise, you wouldn't have shown your low level of knowledge of the history of this great nation. People's rights to consume alcohol were taken away about a hundred years ago, and years later another amendment was passed to restore that constitutional right.

YY: Is there a right in the Constitution for us to consume alcohol or heroin?

SW: Professor, maybe you can clear up something that caught my attention days ago, but I didn't get my thoughts arranged well enough to ask you a good question. You have said that the gun culture in our country was originally brought from England; then it was kept in order to defend the new land and later, the country, from foreign invaders such as England. But then, after the War of 1812–15, one of the reasons to maintain that culture was to be able to fight government oppression. Also, during all that time, people in some parts of the new land had to worry about Indians and/or pirate-type intruders entering their homes and stealing stuff, and now guns are also used just for protection from intruders. So, if we no longer have to worry about foreign

Rx: Emily and Mark, I have to reluctantly agree with you on this. I want to be supportive of all law enforcers, but sometimes, it's hard to do that. Like ET, I'm going to be leaving the room shortly. I'll start putting together some pertinent information regarding the drug industry and the misuse of drugs. Don't conflate my agreement with regard to the Uvalde tragedy with anything else on which you libs think I should agree with you.

KO: Before this class is dismissed, I know Rx hates this, but I'd like to suggest an assignment to all. We have tentatively accepted segments to follow up on. Why don't we each write a summary or outline, as comprehensive as we can, about what aspects within our segments we wish to pursue? We can email our outlines to each other so we can be aware of what will be included and perhaps what we are not covering. Then, after perusing each other's outlines, we can exchange ideas and send inquiries or suggestions to each other.

YY: What a substantial suggestion, Professor! I feel that we are making some real progress if we do this assignment.

PM: Great assignment, Roberto! I'll start creating my outline tomorrow.

SW: Yes, I agree. We've already discussed a lot of facts, reasons, and narratives regarding the subject. Now it's time to get more organized. Let's do it.

Rx: I see you've acquired agreement from your sycophantic students, Prof. Well, I'm not one of them. I don't wish to read a Ph.D.-long dissertation from you.

ET: Clyde, all Roberto has suggested we do is each make an outline, a somewhat concise summary of what we will include in our segments. I'm sure you must have created at least one outline in your extensive studies - it's not a doctoral dissertation. Get onboard. We'll need the segment on drug use and its effect on the mental stability or health of prospective shooters. With that said, I'm now exiting the room to prepare for dinner. Oh gosh! It's already past my dinner time.

PM: Good, gentle retort, Emily. Of course, Clyde, we need your expert knowledge when it comes to narcotics of all types, legal and illegal. We know that lots of street gang murders are drug-related and over money as well. How can we overcome addictions? Should we make some illegal drugs legal under more control and management? Do we simply rely too much on medications versus nutrition, therapy, good habits, and…

Rx: Okay, stop your prodding. I'll consider doing some reviewing and research, but I don't want KO to grade my submission. I'm also leaving, you bubbleheads.

YY: Thanks, Roberto, for elaborating in more detail on what Clyde told us.

SW: Professor, maybe you can clear up something that caught my attention days ago, but I didn't get my thoughts arranged well enough to ask you a good question. You have said that the gun culture in our country was originally brought from England; then it was kept in order to defend the new land and later, the country, from foreign invaders such as England. But then, after the War of 1812–15, one of the reasons to maintain that culture was to be able to fight government oppression. Also, during all that time, people in some parts of the new land had to worry about

Indians and/or pirate-type people breaking into their homes and stealing stuff, and now guns are also used just for protection from intruders. So, if we no longer have to worry about foreign invaders or Indians, and since, other than the Civil War, people haven't had to fight off government oppression in over 200 years, then we are left with one reason to own a gun: home protection. And since you or Mark revealed we are safer without a gun in our home, it seems it would be very easy to convince most people that there's no need to own a gun. To me, it appears to be a concentric circle of a lot of arguments and justifications, each contradicting the others. Am I making any sense?

Rx: See-Saw, what you just took up a lot of time trying to inquire about is antithetical to all the facts relating to crime in our country that have been regurgitated many times over the past several weeks in our Zoom sessions. You invoke KO's words as the only authority for the truth too much!

ET: Shahzad, are you basically reasoning that most of the rational reasons people have given for gun ownership have gone by the wayside? If statistically accurate, having a gun in your home is potentially more harmful than not having one, your reasoning is sound. However, we'd still need to deal with bearing arms, concealed or otherwise, and, of course, hunters and target shooters. Have we all decided and committed ourselves to one or more of the segments we need to research in depth on these very complex issues? As days go by, there are more mass shootings and a variety of other homicides. I still get emotional about that teacher who was lying on the floor of his classroom in Uvalde, Texas, having been shot by the young man who came into his schoolroom and shot all his students, who were also lying on the floor for over an hour while the police were outside the room in the hallway, fully armed and not entering the classroom, while some of those children could have possibly been saved. I'm going to leave the room in a short while, but I hope all of you can cover all the aspects of the gun violence issue we have been discussing so that perhaps we can then share our research and conclusions with a larger group of people.

PM: I can empathize with you, Emily. With the training law enforcement units received after Columbine, those officers should have known the protocols.

SW: Yeah, I think we've got a plan in place! We all need to work hard to cover all the aspects of our sectors. That's a lot of ground to cover, and in my case, I'm going to have to search for a vision and create a realistic approach, one with incentives to stop buying guns and to give them up. My thanks to all of you for taking on this seemingly insurmountable task to save lives! Bye!

KO: My thanks, too, to all of you for getting onboard with the "assignment." I also need to start using my brain more than I've used it in years. Take care.

YY: It's just you and me, Mark. Good luck with the mountain you'll be climbing.

CHAPTER TWELVE

During the early morning hours of Thursday, Roberto, while lying in his bed, began thinking about the new phase his friends in the Zoom chatroom were undertaking. He had already put together his outline, but he assumed most of the others had not. The bigger issue was what they were going to do with the finished project after they had filled in their outlines with substantial information. Would they post their work on social media? Send the information to gun safety organizations? Or maybe have their work published in a book? He couldn't go back to sleep after going through all of those concerns.

ET: I hope someone comes into the room soon. I've been here ten minutes.

Rx: Here I am. You know those guys in California are always tardy. It's only a few minutes past 2 p.m. PST there. They've probably just finished lunch, whereas we have to start thinking about dinner.

PM: Hold on, Clyde. Before you start ragging on us West Coasters, you East Coasters are the ones who ditch us early most often.

ET: Hi, Mark. How are you? Clyde does have a point, spoken sarcastically, of course, that it's a bit late in the afternoon, even dark at some points in the year, when the room opens up.

SW: Good afternoon, everybody. It's good to see all of you again. Mark, did you forget to shave the past few days? Ha ha! Did any of you make any headway with your segment outline? I put some time into mine but didn't get far so far. I must design mine from scratch.

KO: I dreamt about you guys last night. I know some might characterize that as a nightmare, but it wasn't. It just affected my sound sleep.

Rx: What an entrance! Not a "hi" or "good afternoon," just a nightmare.

ET: I did begin to put some of my thoughts down to create my outline. There is a lot to consider in the segment I selected. Even though it's in my field of study and work, I can't imagine how long it's going to take to fill in an outline for your segment, Shahzad, with a comprehensive look at everything.

YY: Hey, everybody, you're all looking good! I just got off a Zoom chat with a business friend of mine who was in Highland Park, Ohio, when that mass killing took place. He said he'd never seen so many people so shaken up.

PM: Okay, Shahzad, your eyesight is still pretty good. Sometimes when I don't need to go out for a couple of days, I don't shave.

Rx: Hey, yo-yo—I mean Yakety-Yak—there you go again. You seem to have friends who are at every mass shooting: Las Vegas and now Highland Park. Where's the next shooting going to take place? You need to send a friend there. Please don't include me in your list of friends!

KO: Clyde, you're the epitome of animus. Your ad hominem attacks are disruptive and very insulting. Why couldn't you just say to Yoshi, "That was a terrible mass shooting your friend witnessed"?

PM: While we are conversing today, about 106 Americans died by guns. It seems that number, and those people's lives, are more important than insulting each other.

ET: Okay, gentlemen, I have something more important to say. You know the name of this chat room is Octogenarians Opine. We have often stated our opinions and views and offered judgments about lots of issues. Now, if we are to move into a higher level of discourse to persuade others, possible readers of our written words, we need to deal in facts and truth. We must think more and feel less.

KO: Emily, your words are so insightful. I'll tell you another person who used words of wisdom such as yours to make a similar point: John F. Kennedy, who stated, "Too often we rely on the comfort of opinion rather than the discomfort of facts. We should not just go with our feelings, but use thoughts based on the research we uncover."

YY: Domo arigatō gozaimasu—oops! I mean, thank you very much, Roberto and Emily, for the distinction and insight between opinions and reality.

SW: Yes, I agree. Now, perhaps we can move forward with truth, facts, and reality on our side.

RX: I'm totally perplexed, yo and See-Saw, over convoluted statements. SW, when you told us about that tower building at the University of Texas in 1966, were you telling us facts or your views? YY, when you told us about your friend who was near the Mandalay Casino and was very depressed, was that just your opinion, or was that reality? I have been accepting what you and the other Zoomers in the room have been saying and responding to your words as being true facts. Have I been duped or brainwashed? KO, your high-minded insults aren't endearing you to me. Be careful.

PM: Clyde, you don't have to try to shame Shahzad and Yoshi because you have disparate thoughts. I think they were just responding to the clarity that Roberto and Emily offered. We should certainly take things as seriously as we can, with respect to passing on what we've learned to others.

RX: When you guys want to fool around with outlines and the prospect that somehow what you learn in your research you are going to pass on that knowledge to other people, there are already tons of information out there in the news. Fox News has stories about crime in big cities every night, and there are lots of books, newspaper articles, audiobooks, documentaries, and TV cop shows about all the aspects of gun violence in this country that we've been talking about. What's new? Why are you wasting your time and energy believing you can excel where others haven't been capable of doing it? That sounds narcissistic to me.

KO: Clyde, it sounds like your logic has bona fides and is convincing, except that it overlooks the concept of progression. In human history, as I'm sure you understand in pharmacology, medications and drugs are introduced on top of other pharmaceuticals to create greater success in treatment. The research continues, and I don't think you believe the researchers are all narcissists. Even with all the information out in public, that doesn't mean no one should attempt to submit more information that updates what exists, has a different focus, or is created in a manner that attracts different people, including politicians, or is simply motivating to activists.

ET: Clyde, you watch Fox News. If that network is one of your sources for factual information, I think we should also talk and think about ways of verifying what is included in our segments. We shouldn't want anything released by our group that can't be verified by reputable sources.

RX: ET, don't knock Fox News! More people watch Tucker Carlson than any other news show on TV. He does have credibility with his gigantic viewership.

YY: Clyde, I beg to differ with you regarding Carlson's viewership numbers. I usually watch David Muir on ABC. According to what I just looked up, his audience numbers for prime-time evening news are over 7 million, whereas Tucker's are just over 4 million. That's why we need to verify the facts we present, as Emily so correctly encouraged us to do.

RX: Yakety-Yak, you had to know I was referring to cable news networks like that abominable CNN and that socialist, woke network MSNBC.

YY: I'm sorry, Clyde, but your words were "any other news show on TV." ABC is on my TV.

KO: What would be the point in presenting nonfactual information? People would quickly try to verify it and then discredit the whole of whatever we have presented. That would be a waste of our time and make us out to be fools, and our arguments for reforms would be harder to sell in the future.ET: Roberto, have you begun to write your segment outline? I don't know about you gentlemen, but I'm motivated to get started on creating my outline and then doing the research I'll need to do to fill in that outline. By the way, I recently learned about a gun manufacturer that is making AR-15–style guns for kids. The guns are a bit smaller and lighter in weight. A preschool-age kid could handle one. They are real guns! They're called JR-15, like junior. We can chat all day, or we can get to work to prevent kids from growing up in a violent gun culture, which is America.

KO: Yes, Emily, I have. I don't wish to put pressure on anyone, but I feel an urgency, both intellectual and marketing, to study and create some suggestions, recommendations, or better yet, a vision for some substantial solutions to help in some way. I agree about your motivation to act now. I hadn't heard about the JR-15.

Rx: KO, you just brought up this idea at our last chat session, and now you are springing this news on us. ET's and your speed and pushiness are rude and flabbergasting, to say the least. I haven't even given my part any consideration yet. Patience!

SW: Maybe we should all check out of the room and get to work on our projects. The thought of little kids having real AR-15–style guns is nauseating. I'm pretty much in the dark about my design. What is this country going to be like without a Second Amendment?

PM: Shahzad, you might benefit by searching online with that question. Perhaps check what it is like in other countries without a Second Amendment. We should devote as much spare time as we have to developing our assigned segments. Emily, the Junior, or JR-15, was introduced last year. It looks like the manufacturers want kids to get enthusiastic about guns at an early age, so they'll buy many guns during their lifetimes.

ET: I agree. Best wishes working on this very important project. Bye now.

YY: I'll use this Zoom time to contemplate and reflect on my segment subject.

KO: Looks like that's the plan now. We can't fail. Too many lives are at stake.

CHAPTER THIRTEEN

Two weeks had passed. Emily missed dialoguing with her Zoom room friends and sent them an email requesting that they schedule a Zoom meeting. They all agreed to the date, so she scheduled the time and opened the room at 5 p.m. East Coast time.

Rx: Is anyone other than me in this room yet? I don't have a lot of time to chat this evening.

ET: Hi, Clyde. How are you? I've missed you guys. How are you doing with your project? Or maybe I shouldn't inquire.

SW: Glad someone is in the room already. Good afternoon. It seems like a month has gone by since we last met.

Rx: To answer your inquiry, ET, I haven't had a lot of time to devote to the project, but what I've uncovered has been a little interesting. Drugs are a wide-ranging subject, as you probably know, with lots of variables and uses.
(After a phone call from Emily, ten minutes later)

KO: Buenas tardes, amigos. Oops, I should say "good afternoon, friends" to please Clyde and be clear to Shahzad and Yoshi.

PM: Good afternoon, everybody. You sure get into this Zoom room quickly. What's happening?

SW: To answer your question, Emily, the more I reflect on our project, the deeper into the weeds I get. When I look at mental health issues, prisons, hate, and racism, there are also issues with parenting, schools, and poverty. And maybe many of the shooters were born with some kind of genetic issue related to violence.

ET: Shahzad, you've covered a lot of ground there. The genetics issue is brilliant.

PM: I think one of the defendants in a case in my department tried to use that as a defense.

ET: I'll definitely look into this in my research.

RX: Let me mull that thought over. Are you trying to proffer that God may be instilling evil genes into fetuses? That distortion of reality would surely provide pro-abortion activists an excuse to terminate pregnancies.

KO: It sounds as though you have been putting in some time, Shahzad, trying to come up with your outline. I have developed mine to the extent that I am ready to offer it to all of you to scrutinize and consider any suggestions.

PM: I'm glad you've gotten that far, Roberto. I've put together most of my outline, and I'd like to see yours and perhaps get some ideas from it to complete mine pretty soon.

Rx: I don't know if you heard what I said before. I think we're all doing something with our outlines, but just don't try to give me an ultimatum; that's problematic for me. We have other aspects of our lives we need to deal with.

ET: That's a good idea you have, Roberto. Yes, send what you've created. I'm coming up with so many pieces of information and research that it's hard to put it all into a concise package at this time. I'll need more time to compile it and work through it all.

KO:	Okay, I'll send it as an attachment in an email in the next day or so. Please feel free to comment, criticize it, or offer suggestions for more inclusion or whatever. Thanks, everyone, even Clyde. When you're ready to discuss it, please send me a text or an email so we can carry on.

PM:	That stimulates me to get moving more on my outline and finish it. I'll be back in the room next Tuesday at our usual time. I hope some of you will join Roberto and me then. Good luck, everyone, with your outlines. We've just got to keep being conscious of just how vital our efforts may be in saving lives and our country as well. See you later, everyone.

YY:	Thanks for texting, Mark. I would have missed this entire session. I'll look forward to reading your outline, Roberto, and I'll keep probing for more information on the international circumstances and data. I'll come back into the room next Tuesday, as Mark mentioned. Sayonara.

ET:	I'm thrilled that some real progress is on the horizon. Every time there is a school shooting, I'm depressed that there's no real movement to prevent another one. We can't hire thousands of former police officers and vets to guard all our schools, all 50 million students. Thanks, Roberto. I'll surely read your outline and respond to you. And I'll be back in our room Tuesday. Take care, everyone!

SW:	Thanks a lot, Roberto.

CHAPTER FOURTEEN

He had finally completed the draft of his segment outline. It was as difficult as any report he had ever written while working in law enforcement. He had sent it as an email to all his Zoom chatroom partners before going to bed Monday night. Now it was 2 p.m. PST, and he was ready to take Clyde's criticism and praise from Emily and probably all the others.

PM: Hello, anybody joining me?

YY: Hi, Mark, you're so prompt. Did you learn that trait while being a policeman? I got your outline, and at first glance, it looks thorough.

ET: Hi, friends and compadres. Oops, I should wait and let Roberto use that word. I'm glad you are including domestic violence and proper storage of firearms, Mark. Women and children must be protected from guns being in households.

KO: Say, Mark, I can definitely see your background coming through your outline. It's impressive! Including the social media aspect to be researched when it comes to mass shootings is crucial to our understanding of why young men are so involved in those incidents. Emily, it's fine with me whenever an English speaker uses a Spanish word. The more often a foreign-language word is used in our country, the more it will be understood.

Rx: Your 2(C) and 2(E) are worthy of our consideration, but 2(F), oh, hi, Mark. Militias may have guns, but they're not like street drug gangs shooting at each other. They believe they have a legitimate purpose for their existence.

PM: Thanks, one and all, for reviewing my outline. I know there will be other aspects that will pop up or that you folks will bring to my attention.

SW: Howdy, everyone! Mark, you've got a lot of structure to navigate through with all those law enforcement agencies and jurisdictions. If there's any one of us who would be able to do it, it's you.

KO: Clyde, I'd think you would also be delving into the narcotics trafficking issue. We all know how impactful that is in our country.

Rx: I don't have to be told that, KO. I'll see if I have time to spend dealing with that element in my segment.

YY: With Roberto's segment covering some of the important aspects of the development of guns, the culture of gun usage brought to the colonies, the creation and inclusion of the Second Amendment, and Mark and Roberto dealing with laws and enforcement, a good foundation is being put in place for understanding the situation we're in. However, we've got many miles to go to come up with a deeper understanding of our violent gun culture.

Rx: With all your rambling, are we to conclude you'll be the next one to submit a segment outline?

SW: Well said, Yoshi. I don't think you or I should go next. With you focusing on the international scene and me focusing on the post–Second Amendment scene in America, that just boils down to Clyde and Emily. Does my reasoning make sense?

ET: Yes, your reasoning is solid as far as I'm concerned. Knowing of Doctor Clyde's foot-dragging techniques and busy schedule, I'm willing to step up to the plate and be next to submit my segment outline. I'll need a week or two to accomplish this task.

KO: Thanks, Emily, for stepping up to the plate next. Mark and I know how time-consuming and stressful it is to collect the information needed, put it into a plausible order, and try to cover all the important elements in the segment.

YY: Your segment on mental health and related aspects of gun violence will give our project a new perspective and feel to it. I look forward to seeing what you write. I'm sure I'll learn a lot. Thanks, Emily!

PM: Well, let's close out this session before you guys get back to picking on the outline.

SW: Thanks again, Mark, for your professional look at all the complications of law enforcement as it pertains to gun violence.

Roberto Alvarez Outline

1. The Second Amendment to the Bill of Rights was adopted in 1791.

    A. Background and reasons for it.

    B. Need for guns for protection from foreign invaders, Native Americans, and westward expansion.

    C. Response from the citizenry.

2. States were not happy that the federal government had the final say regarding interpretation.

3. In 1875, in the case of U.S. v. Cruikshank, the primary holding of the Court was that the Second Amendment does not bar states from regulating firearms because, irrespective of that amendment, people have a right to own and bear firearms.

4. Supreme Court decisions and other legal challenges to it.

5. Federal gun laws influenced by the undemocratic majority makeup of the U.S. Senate, where every state, such as Wyoming, has an equal two votes with California.

6. Gun ownership and rights lobby organizations, such as the NRA.

7. History of gun culture and ownership by regions.

8. Changing reasons for gun ownership and bearing arms, and reasons for stricter laws in the country's history.

CHAPTER FIFTEEN

It was a very long weekend for everyone. They had read about or seen news stories about more gun violence in the U.S. "Please send your thoughts and prayers," was said by the chief of police at a microphone following the revealing of details about the shooting. Then came Tuesday, 4:55 p.m. EDT.

ET: "I'm in our room now… " was the text she sent to the group.

KO: Hi, Emily. You beat me to the punch on my phone key to send a text to everyone. Did you enjoy your weekend?

ET: Thanks for asking. Yes, I did, mostly the time I spent reading your outline.

RX: KO, your conceptualization of our project hit extreme heights in your outline.

PM: Hi, all. How so, Clyde?

Rx: KO could write a 200-page book with all the expansive aspects he is proposing to include in his segment. If we all cover that much ground, in book form, it would be over 1,000 pages. Let's keep it readable and understandable.

SW: I appreciate that you, Roberto, cover over 400 years of American history. The period prior to 1791 is very important to understand. I'm sure I'm going to learn a lot from your segment.

ET: Yes, Shahzad, I'm also interested in what Roberto includes in the historical part, especially when it comes to Plymouth Rock versus Jamestown. One was for freedom of religion, and one was entrepreneurial-based.

KO: Clyde, I understand your concerns and appreciate your input. One of the thoughts I kept having as I did my research was that we must try to reach as many people with our arguments as possible: different ages, regional cultures, political biases, education levels, professions, income levels, immigrants, etc.

YY: Congratulations, professor! Your outline is so comprehensive and interesting. I'm afraid my segment outline is going to look like it was written by a kindergartner next to yours.

Rx: KO, you included things that are settled and part of our Constitution and won't be changed, such as the bicameral legislature we have in the federal government. Wyoming isn't going to relinquish its two Senate seats, no matter how unfair it is to California. We should just incorporate items in our segments that can possibly be changed or modified and keep it short so folks won't look at our production and be daunted by its length or avoid reading any of it.

KO: Good point and argument, Clyde. I'll reconsider that item and double check other items. Anyone else with a point of view???

SW: Roberto, with my segment dealing with the possible post–Second Amendment era in the U.S., shouldn't I start out covering the repeal of the amendment and all the circumstances involved in that transition?

KO: Another good point, Shahzad. Perhaps we can both cover it somewhat. You can, if you wish, cover the resistance to the repeal. There will be a lot of it, and it may prove to be threatening to our democracy. Once we write our segments, maybe we can blend the two. So I'd suggest that you go ahead and cover what you wish about the demise of the amendment.

Rx: Get real! The repeal will only happen after another civil war in this country.

PM: I have almost completed my first draft of my outline. Maybe I should send it at the end of this week. With the stuff Roberto's going to be considering, I don't want to put too much time into mine only to have it shredded by Clyde.

YY: Mark, are you going to be dealing with the enforcement of the gun laws and the misuse of guns? Are you going to include using the National Guard to enforce laws?

PM: Yes, Yoshi, I'll be covering those things and more. There's a multitude of confusion about what to enforce, with various court interpretations and the multitude of law enforcement agencies dealing with state and federal legislation and court decisions. Good question regarding the National Guard.

ET: Best wishes, Mark! It looks like you've got a full plate to deal with. However, I'm sure your law enforcement background will sustain you in your efforts. I'll look forward to seeing your outline this weekend. On that note, gentlemen, I'm going to say good night.

Rx: Yeah, I've got to take care of some business. The Constitution won't be changed in areas such as the bicameral legislature we have in the federal government. Wyoming isn't going to relinquish its two Senate seats. In our segments, we should focus on what can possibly be changed or modified and keep it short so folks won't look at our production and be daunted by its length or discouraged from reading any of it.

KO: Good point and argument, Clyde. I'll reconsider that item and double-check other items. Anyone else with a point of view?

SW: Roberto, with my segment dealing with the possible post–Second Amendment era in the U.S., shouldn't I start out covering the repeal of the amendment and all the circumstances involved in that transition?

KO: Another good point, Shahzad. Perhaps we can both cover it somewhat. You can, if you wish, cover the resistance to the repeal. There'll be a lot of it, and it may prove to be threatening to our democracy. Once we write our segments, maybe we can blend the two. So I'd suggest that you go ahead and cover what you wish about the demise of the amendment.

Rx: Get real! The repeal will only happen after another civil war in this country.

PM: I have almost completed my first draft of my outline. Maybe I should send it at the end of this week. With the stuff Roberto's going to be considering, I don't want to put too much time into mine only to have it shredded.

YY: Mark, are you going to be dealing with the enforcement of the gun laws and the misuse of guns? Are you going to include using the National Guard to enforce laws?

PM: Yes, Yoshi, I'll be covering those things and more. There's a multitude of confusion about what to enforce, with various court interpretations and the multitude of law enforcement agencies dealing with state and federal legislation and court decisions. Good question regarding the National Guard.

ET: Best wishes, Mark! It looks like you've got a full plate to deal with. However, I'm sure your law enforcement background will sustain you in your efforts. I'll look forward to seeing your outline this weekend. On that note, gentlemen, I'm going to say good night.

Rx: Yeah, I've got to take care of some business.

Emily Thurmond's outline

A. Segment Category: Mental Illness / Health

   1. General illnesses related to gun violence
   2. Childhood trauma
   3. Signs of mental disorders
   4. Services available in counties/schools

B. Red Flag Laws

   1. What to report to authorities
   2. Need for reporting
   3. Help that can be offered
   4. Prevention of gun violence, including suicide

C. Cultural Influences Affecting the Provocation of Gun Use

   1. Racism
   2. Movies, songs
   3. Social media
   4. Video games
   5. Manufacturers' marketing appeals to young men/ promotions

D. Domestic Violence

   1. Relationship problems
   2. Counseling for problems
   3. Statistics when a gun is in the home
   4. Fear/living with a threat

E. Treatments

   1. Intervention from families
   2. Social services available

3. Marriage and family counseling
4. Rehabilitation treatment
5. Anger management

F. Legal Remedies

1. Restraining orders
2. House of Ruth
3. Separation/divorce
4. Hotline for domestic abuse/violence

CHAPTER SIXTEEN

She wasn't used to fidgeting, but Emily had to control her hands and thoughts as she awaited the 5:00 p.m. EST time. She had looked forward to discussing mental health issues with her Zoom chatroom partners. Between mental health issues and drug addiction, which could conceivably fall under the same umbrella, far too many Americans have been revealing the devastation of those problems in the country. Oops, the timer went off.

ET: Hello, it's time to show your faces after a week and a half.

YY: You look just the same, Emily. I hope I do too. I see you've been hard at work creating your masterpiece segment outline.

Rx: There you go again, Yakety Yak. Emily, your work does deserve some praise, but "masterpiece" seems to be going overboard.

KO: It's back to class after some vacation time—except for Emily. Your knowledge of the mental health field is revealed well in your impressive outline.

SW: Good afternoon, everyone. With the U.S. having about 44 percent of all the earth's recorded suicides currently, it makes this a very vital issue, considering also that half the suicides in the U.S. are caused by guns.

PM: I see you're on the beat again. Hi, everyone. That's significant data you're raising, Shahzad. Your outline is full of significant points, but I'm most interested in section C and racism and social media in particular.

You don't look as though you have been stressed out, having worked tirelessly over the past ten days or so.

KO: In regard to the social media subject, have you ever counseled a teenager about being on social media too much, or parents who needed help dealing with a child who was on social media too much on a daily basis, Emily?

ET: Hi, Roberto and Mark. To answer your question, Roberto, I haven't had clients in over a dozen years. The current social media rage wasn't raising its challenging head as it is now. Parents back then often took much more control of their kids' cell phones.

YY: Emily, you brought up a very significant point regarding violent and aggressive behavior being a biological problem that can be dealt with. Remember, the cells, or whatever they are, were more concentrated in the prefrontal area of the brain. I don't see anything about that feature in your outline. Are you going to cover that?

Rx: Yakety Yak, ET's got that birth issue covered in her red flag stuff. Look carefully and you'll see the word "prevention."

ET: Yoshi, I'm glad you took note of that neurological deformity issue. That may someday prove to be a major prevention method to reduce violent behavior. I'll spell it out more clearly in my revised draft. Thank you very much! Any more brilliant observations? Clyde, shush!

PM: I'll be interested to see what you come up with dealing with childhood trauma. I witnessed many terrible incidents involving kids during my years on duty. It's unimaginable and incredible how low humanity can sink when it involves children.

SW: We've now had three impressive and vital component segment outlines presented. I may be rushing things, yet it seems we need another volunteer to put his head on the chopping block. I'm sorry, that's probably too crude. Any takers?

YY: Well, there are only three of us non-presenters left. From all I've heard the doc state, he won't be forced to expedite his outline, and as discussed previously, you, Shahzad, have the lineage topic that logically comes as the final link of our segments. You like structure, Shahzad, so this reasoning appeals to you, right? I'll do it.

Rx: You're finally making sense, Yakety Yak, I mean businessman, Yoshi.

SW: From your words, Yoshi, one can draw only one conclusion as to who's next on the chopping block: YOU! Go to it.

KO: Your reasoning meets my approval, Yoshi. It should be fun, to some extent, studying other countries and comparing differences in culture, parenting, schools, gun laws, drugs, mental health, and other related components of their societies to compare with ours.

Yoshi's outline

1. Countries that have a constitutional right, a Second Amendment–type right, to keep and bear arms, like the United States.

2. Gun ownership and homicide rates in other countries with Second Amendment–type constitutional laws.

3. Developed countries that don't allow citizens to own and bear arms: homicide statistics and other data.

4. Developed countries that do allow firearm ownership: ownership statistics and homicide rates.

5. Restrictive laws and requirements for buying and owning guns in some countries, such as permits, registration, and licensing.

6. Countries without Second Amendment–type laws that have high gun ownership with restrictions: Switzerland, Finland, Japan, etc.

7. Countries with concealed or open carry of firearms: permits required? Types of firearms that can be carried in public.

8. Countries with the lowest homicide rates and no gun violence: gun-ownership laws.

9. Incarceration and rehabilitation in developed countries: How are education, parenting, and prison rehabilitation programs different from those in the U.S.?

10. How do homicide rates in developed countries differ from those in the U.S.?

11 How is social media different in low-homicide, developed countries than in the U.S.?

12. Problems between other countries and the U.S. due to the gun manufacturing industry in the U.S.

13. Differences in drug use, demographics, mental health, and suicide issues between the U.S. and other developed countries.

Rx: I'm sure we'll see a lot of applauding of how fantastic the gun handling is in Japan. Spare us an overabundance of hype.

ET: There you go again, spewing disparaging remarks. Yoshi, I, for one, will be eagerly awaiting what your research uncovers.

SW: I think you've mentioned countries besides Japan that you've already looked at. Will you be checking out Iran?

YY: I've looked at information regarding Switzerland, Finland, and Japan. Okay, Shahzad, I'll see what I can find on Iran.

KO: I've followed firearm ownership laws in the UK since the colonists brought England's gun culture to America in the 1600s. It's really ironic that the U.S. has a Second Amendment right to own and bear arms, but the UK doesn't have any written right like that.

Rx: KO, are you attempting to usurp Yakety Yak's outline already?

YY: Thanks for that piece of info, Roberto. I haven't looked at the UK yet. It's interesting that they have changed their gun culture so much.

PM: Another aspect the doc may criticize is that most police officers in England don't carry weapons, only special units do. Item 8 should be eye-opening to Americans: countries with little or no gun laws allow gun ownership and yet have low homicide rates.

ET: We can continue praising and asking questions of Yoshi, but I think we should move our project along by making some plans.

PM: Do you have any suggestions for plans?

ET: We have three options: Shahzad can present his segment outline soon, Clyde can present his outline, or Roberto can present a section of his segment for perusal and discussion.

SW: Knowing the doc as I do, I don't see option two as viable. We may get ahead of ourselves with Roberto showing some of his work. So that leaves only option one, and I'll commit to being next. Just as all who have submitted outlines requested, I'll do the same. Give me two or three weeks to put my thoughts and imagination into an organized and understandable format.

KO: Your reasoning is sound, it always is, Shahzad. The three weeks will give those of us who already have our outlines time to work on our segments.

Clyde Graf, PharmD
Outline of Drugs

1. Definition of drugs/narcotics

2. History of drugs/narcotics

3. What makes a drug legal in the U.S.

4. What makes a drug illegal in the U.S.

5. FDA and regulatory determinations

6. Pharmaceutical industry in the U.S.

7. Benefits and detriments of drug usagew

8. Disposal of unused drugs

9. Importation of drugs: legal and illegal

10. Government agencies and enforcement of laws

11. Black market

12. Drug gangs and crime involving narcotics

13. Definition of drug addiction and effects therefrom

14. Chances for long-term sobriety from addiction

CHAPTER SEVENTEEN

Three and a half weeks had passed since he asked for time off to write his outline, and now it was as complete as he could make it at this time. So, he sent his fellow committee members his outline as an email attachment and told them he would be back in the Zoom chatroom the following Thursday. It was nearly 4:00 p.m. Central Time when he entered the room.

SW: Hi, friends, I'm here and ready to discuss my thoughts in my outline. (A few moments transpired.)

ET: Good afternoon, Shahzad. You're looking calm and peaceful, having gone through the mental stress you may have experienced lately.

SW: Good to see you again, Emily. Thanks for the good observation. I feel fine now that I've given my best to making the outline. I know improvements can be added, so I'm open to suggestions.

ET: It seems to me that the almost insurmountable challenge will be getting the courts to repeal the amendment. We'll need a very forward-looking court with justices who have come to the point of determining that far too many lives have been lost due to a misinterpretation of the Second Amendment years ago.

Rx: You two are hallucinating again. No way will the Supreme Court repeal the Second Amendment!!!

ET: Welcome to the room, Clyde. We were about ready to miss your sarcasm.

PM: Congratulations, Shahzad! Your outline is well conceived. If I may, however, even with all the new restrictions, buybacks, and liability changes for manufacturers, there will still be about 300 million guns in the hands of Americans, including about 25 million owners of AR-15–style rifles.

KO: Thanks, Shahzad, for your efforts to move our collaboration along. Mark makes a very strong argument that nothing significant can really be done with so many weapons already in our country. It's estimated that we have nearly 50 percent of all privately owned guns in the entire world.

YY: Good afternoon, everyone. Sorry I'm a bit late. I won't try to explain why. Emily, I heard part of your point about the court's misinterpretation of the Second Amendment's two clauses. I think it was you, Roberto, who told us that it was Justice Scalia who separated the two clauses, making the first one, dealing with the militias, irrelevant.

KO: Your memory is still intact, Yoshi. It was I who presented that two weeks ago. The new misinterpretation occurred in the Supreme Court's Heller decision in 2008.

SW: I'll need to get into that in my segment dealing with the repeal of the Second Amendment. Maybe, Roberto, you can send me some info on that decision.

Rx: You guys are wasting your time thinking the Second Amendment can be repealed. See Saw, why are you getting into the "radical," left-wing cultural nonsense stuff?

YY: It might be enlightening if we found a grammarian scholar who could definitively inform us of the interaction of the two clauses and whether the second clause is solely based upon the first clause.

Rx: Yakety Yak, you're getting close to jumping off a cliff or taking a fentanyl tablet if you continue to proceed with your wild speculations.

KO: Yoshi, good idea. I could consult with one of my colleagues who teaches grammar for an opinion.

ET: I always feel guilty bringing up the thought of making future plans; however, as you all know, it's already past 6 p.m. on the East Coast and time for dinner. You guys can go on without my participation, or we can make some plans.

Rx: It's past 6 p.m. for me too. I can surmise what you guys must be assuming now regarding future plans. Don't be mistaken, even though you've all submitted outlines and I haven't, I don't plan to expedite writing mine. I've done some research, but I've got a lot more to do.

PM: I suggest that we work on our segments when Clyde finishes his outline, and he can send all of us an email when he's ready to show it to us. Hopefully, it will be this calendar year. See you then.

Rx: Ha ha, PM. Okay. *Verabschiedung!*

CHAPTER EIGHTEEN

Yoshi spent the evening sitting on his balcony with his wife, Kikue, looking at the beautiful sunset from his house on a cliff over the horizon of the Pacific Ocean waves, talking about what he had learned in his search for information in other countries. She was curious and asked him many questions. He had decided during his research and conversations that he had missed out on a lot of traveling Kikue had taken with friends.

YY: Put on your boxing gloves, Clyde. I'm ready to take a punch.

KO: Hey, Yoshi, you've got a lot of geography to cover in your segment research. I'm interested in the difference in gun culture by continent. Do Asian countries have less homicide per capita, or do European countries? What does Africa look like versus South America?

YY: That's interesting, Roberto. I'll see if I can find data on continents as a whole.

RX: YY, your numbers 9 and 13 cover too many issues and subjects. You'll need a year to research all of that and 100 pages or more to report on your findings. You were waiting for a knockout punch, and here it is.

SW: Good afternoon, everybody. Your outline is impressive, Yoshi. I kind of wonder whether some countries, like Russia, China, and Iran, release authentic data instead of propaganda to make themselves look better.

YY: That's a good point, Shahzad. Hi. I will attempt to obtain figures from a variety of sources.

PM: Good glorious afternoon, one and all. I hope I didn't miss much. I didn't miss the doc's remarks. Clyde, I thought using a lot of time didn't trouble you, so why are you concerned about Yoshi taking a year for his research? He's got some very pertinent points to cover. I hope all of you enjoyed yourselves as much as I have lately.

ET: Gee, am I the last one to enter the room? Wow! Yoshi, I'm impressed with your vast-coverage outline. I agree with Mark, you've got some essential areas on which to report. As I may have stated before, cultural aspects such as good parenting, education, employment opportunities, and financial stability are some of the primary issues in having a successful society.

Rx: I'm sure we'll see a lot of applauding of how fantastic the gun handling is in Japan. Spare us an overabundance of hype.

ET: There you go again, spewing disparaging remarks. Yoshi, I, for one, will be eagerly awaiting what your research uncovers.

SW: I think you've mentioned countries besides Japan that you've already looked at. Will you be checking out Iran?

YY: I've looked at information regarding Switzerland, Finland, and Japan. Okay, Shahzad, I'll see what I can find on Iran.

KO: I've followed firearm ownership laws in the UK since the colonists brought England's gun culture to America in the 1600s. It's really ironic that the U.S. has a Second Amendment right to own and bear arms, but the UK doesn't have any written right like that.

Rx: KO, are you attempting to usurp Yakety Yak's outline already?

YY: Thanks for that piece of info, Roberto. I haven't looked at the UK yet. It's interesting that they have changed their gun culture so much.

PM: Another aspect the doc may criticize is that most police officers in England don't carry weapons, only special units do. Item 8 should be eye-opening to Americans: countries with little or no gun laws allow gun ownership and yet have low rates of homicide.

ET: We can continue praising and asking questions of Yoshi, but I think we should move our project along by making some plans.

PM: Do you have any suggestions for plans?

ET: We have three options: Shahzad can present his segment outline soon; Clyde can present his outline; or Roberto can present a section of his segment for perusal and discussion.

SW: Knowing the doc as I do, I don't see option two as viable. We may get ahead of ourselves with Roberto showing some of his work. So that only leaves option one, and I'll commit to being next. Just as all who have submitted outlines requested, I'll do the same. Give me two or three weeks to put my thoughts and imagination into an organized and understandable format.

KO: Your reasoning is sound, it always is, Shahzad. The three weeks will give those of us who have our outlines time to work on our segments.

CHAPTER NINETEEN

Within 24 hours, Clyde had his brief segment outline completed. He didn't want his Zoom adversaries to think he had acquiesced to their pressure; he wanted them to see how efficient, thorough, and succinct he was. He emailed all the Zoom room participants his outline with a time he would be back in the Zoom room, then got himself a Jägermeister to drink on his patio. He waited until 5 p.m. and went into the Zoom room.

Rx: Okay, all you clowns, come into the room and attack my work! (several minutes later)

PM: You must be trying to push our buttons, Clyde. I didn't expect anything from you until Halloween.

Rx: For a cop, you can be fooled.

SW: What's this? An outline? You sure do believe in brevity, Doctor.

YY: Congratulations, Doctor! You are very prompt. I have a question regarding item 9. How do we know that an imported drug is FDA approved? Does our FDA check out imported products to ensure they match exactly the ones the FDA approved?

ET: Clyde, you've caught us off guard with your promptness. Were you just trying to mess with us when you mentioned not expediting the production of your outline? It's brief but somewhat complete. Thank you.

RX: The FDA has to approve all drugs sold in the U.S. legally.

SW: I see you didn't mention supplements. Aren't they drugs?

KO: Wow, you guys have been carrying on for a while. Sorry, I'm late joining you. I didn't expect to hear from you, Clyde, for weeks or perhaps months. I see you have a smirk on your face. I suppose you feel you succeeded in scamming us with your no-ultimatum statement. Anyway, I'm glad you've produced the outline now. Before I get into Clyde's outline, I want to say that I inadvertently omitted something rather important in my outline: our country's first constitution, called the Articles of Confederation, written in 1777, you probably know of it. It mentioned militias governed by the states, but not rights to own and bear firearms. Now, Clyde, I'd like to ask,

RX: Hold it, KO! I'd like to know why the Articles are relevant.

PM: It's been our common courtesy not to interrupt each other.

KO: I'll be glad to answer the question. I'm going to research what the various states had in their constitutions to find what each state was thinking about gun ownership rights before Madison brought the Virginia version of the Second Amendment idea to Congress in 1789.

YY: That sounds like an interesting research project, Roberto.

Rx: Not to me. It sounds like it's irrelevant to our project.

KO: Clyde, are you going to address just how harmful fentanyl is to our country's youth and homeless people? Also, how can we mitigate its effects?

Rx: It sounds like you wish my segment to be long like yours.

ET: That's a very crucial concern for our country to address.

Rx: How is it related to gun ownership?

SW: That's your focus, Clyde. How narcotics are connected to crime, suicide, homelessness, and other gun-ownership issues are the purposes of your segment. Good luck inspiring the country with your wisdom.

PM: Doc, law enforcement personnel across the country will be forever grateful should you create a solution to drug addiction, thus reducing crime and homicides substantially.

Rx: You guys are overbearing. Do you think I'm God? Okay. Developing more powerful, destructive firearms should share lots of the blame for the gun violence we have in our country. That political appointee is just mouthing what his boss in the White House wants him to declare.

PM: That declaration is very important to what we are dealing with. The SG is acknowledging what we all know: that in many parts of our country, one can't walk down a street safely, kids can't be in school 100 percent safe, and women are much more vulnerable to being shot where there is a severe gun violence problem.

ET: I agree with you, Mark. Roberto, thanks for laying the foundation for our firearms problems. It's the manufacturers who keep developing more powerful, destructive firearms who should share much of the blame for the gun violence we have in our country.

ET: What's good about this SG advisory declaration is that it will provide funds for research, mental health assistance, and other valuable resources for the prevention of this crisis.

Rx: KO, you sure think highly of yourself. It's one thing to provide a historical list of subsets of firearms development over the centuries, but it's quite another to think you are capable of amending one of the most cherished amendments in our Bill of Rights. Have you been diagnosed as narcissistic?

YY: Roberto, you have provided us with plenty of food for thought. Now, can the rest of us make equal contributions to our resolution to create powerful suggestions to ameliorate our extreme gun violence problem in our country?

ET: Clyde, shame on you! Roberto has obviously put a lot of effort and thought into creating his segment. I can tell you from my counseling experience that he's not a narcissistic person. We need bold proposals such as those he has produced.

PM: I agree with Roberto that the Second Amendment needs to be rewritten so that the average person can read it and understand it without having to rely on a judge's interpretation for clarification. If it is okay with all of you, I'll be submitting my segment next. I've been working on it, as most of you have been working on yours.

SW: Thanks, Mark, for volunteering to create and submit the next segment. Unless Emily wishes to do it next, I'm all for you being next in line. Roberto has given us a fabulous segment, and hopefully we can match him somehow in order to meet the challenge we've undertaken.

ET: Thanks, Shahzad, for thinking of me; however I think Mark's segment dealing with law enforcement responsibilities, the laws to enforce, criminal gangs with guns, recidivism, and so forth is a good follow-up to Roberto's segment. Go for it!

KO: Thanks, Mark. I figured you'd step up to the plate next. Your segment seems to be the most logical one to follow mine, in that you'll be dealing with crime involving guns more than the others. I have collected lots of articles, research materials, etc., that I haven't used. If you feel that I may have some information you can use, just let me know. Best wishes in creating a very formidable segment that will influence readers to join us.

YY: Good luck, Mark! I have confidence in your ability and knowledge to create the segment that covers your area of expertise. I'll be eagerly awaiting what you submit.

Rx: Okay, let's see what a rookie cop can produce. Just keep it shorter than KO's presentation.

PM: Thanks, all. See you later.

ROBERTO'S SEGMENT:

<u>Creation and Evolution of Guns up to the Passage of the Second Amendment</u>

Ironically as it may seem, gunpowder was accidentally discovered almost fifteen hundred years ago in China. Due to a wartime situation, the Chinese army, in the tenth century, developed a bamboo tube full of gunpowder that could project a lance, or spear, from it. That was the first firearm.

No one then could have envisioned the monumentally devastating effects firearms would bring upon humanity. Next to natural disasters and invisible viruses, firearms have been the most destructive invention to humankind.

As the Chinese continued defending themselves, their weapons continued to evolve into easier-to-use and more efficient forms. By the fourteenth century, they had developed a weapon called a hand cannon that a man could hold, carry, aim, and fire at an enemy farther away with accuracy.

With gunpowder brought westward into European areas in the thirteenth century, it was not long afterward that hand cannons followed. The French and Germans started using something like the fire lance in the thirteenth century, and the English followed soon after. The French introduced the matchlock, and the Portuguese introduced it to the Chinese.

In the article entitled "Historical Bases of the Right to Keep and Bear Arms," written by David T. Hardy, he says, "…the right to keep and bear arms … is all but impossible to document its actual beginning."

Due to the fact that it was the English who settled on the East Coast of what is now the U.S., looking at Great Britain's history with the concept of the right or requirement to keep and bear arms is most vital to our understanding of what eventually happened in the colonies and the U.S. English kings, instead of having standing armies like most other European nations in the thirteenth, fourteenth, and fifteenth centuries, desired their countrymen to be armed and ready to protect them and maintain their control from within and without the country, with armed reserves of militias that had been around since the tenth century.

<u>Firearms in England</u>

In the early 1500s in England, the weapon of choice was the crossbow. Smaller, shorter firearms called "hand cannons," which could be carried easily, were replacing the crossbow and other former weapons.

Under Elizabeth I's reign, the concept of the militia was used to support the freedom to keep and bear arms. The militias were maintained locally, organized under the supervision of county leaders. They were given the responsibility to protect barons, landowners, government leaders, and, of course, the monarchy.

Under Charles I, in 1636, the militias were still organized and under the control of the kingdom. However, during the civil war between the king's supporters and those supporting Parliament, more militia members became involved on one side or the other. Charles I was overthrown and executed. Under Charles II, an actual British army was created in 1661.

In 1607, the English created a militia in Virginia. By then, Massachusetts had organized a militia in 1636. Some towns and areas in other English colonies also had militias.

Going back to firearms in England, here is information about the most prominent gun used in Europe, the Middle East, and England following the use of the hand cannon. It was called the matchlock and began to be used in England in the early 1400s. It used gunpowder, a cord soaked in flammable liquid, and a burning match to send a bullet up to 650 feet. It took about a minute to reload the nine-pound gun.

Firearms in the colonies

The matchlock musket was popular and used in Jamestown and by the Pilgrims in the colonies. A firearm called the English doglock, which was a rifle and pistol, replaced the matchlock during the period from 1625 to the late 1600s. Later, the flintlock allowed the charge to be loaded at the breech, at the opposite end of the barrel from the muzzle, where shells had previously been loaded.

These early guns began to be created in countries such as Portugal, China, and Japan. In the colonies, the popular firearms were manufactured by Remington, which started producing them in 1816, followed by Smith & Wesson in 1852, Colt in 1855, and Winchester in 1866. Many of these firearms were obviously utilized in the Civil War.

Militias in America

Since the Second Amendment in the Bill of Rights states in its first clause, "A well-regulated Militia, being necessary to the security of a free State," the concept of the militia is an essential factor in the amendment. Looking at the historical elements of that concept is essential to understanding what the Founding Fathers understood it to be when they incorporated it into the amendment.

The idea of citizens keeping and bearing arms had to be a precursor to the creation of militias. British King Henry II created the Assize of Arms rule in 1181, which required all citizens (males only) between fifteen and forty years old to purchase and keep arms (not guns at that time).

In a Wikipedia article on militias, "The modern English term militia dates to the year 1590… There have been changes in the definition…: a military force raised from the civilian population of a country or region, especially to supplement a regular army in an emergency." The U.S. Supreme Court has accepted this definition: "a body of civilians trained to do military duty who may be called out in certain cases, but may be kept on service like standing armies in time of peace."

Today, only Congress has authority over the militia. There is no authority for a group of private citizens to organize and call themselves a militia for the purpose of any military-style service.

Connection of England's Bill of Rights to **the** U.S. Second Amendment

The British Parliament created a Bill of Rights in 1689. Article VII was restrictive, allowing only Protestants to own guns for their own defense. British monarchs retained governing authority over gun rights until the War for Independence began in the colonies on April 19, 1775.

It was not until 1776 that colonies/states in America included that right in their constitutions. Pennsylvania, in September 1776, in its Constitution, Article 43, provided citizens a "right to own and bear arms for their own defense."

The state of Virginia's 1776 Constitution states in Article I, section 13: "That a well-regulated militia, composed of the body of the people, trained to arms, is the proper, natural, and safe defense of a free state; therefore, the right of the people to keep and bear arms shall not be infringed; that standing armies, in time of peace, should be avoided as dangerous to liberty; and that in all cases the militia should be under strict subordination to, and governed by, the civil power."

North Carolina was the only other state that gave citizens a right to keep and bear arms in its December 18, 1776, Constitution before the Articles of Confederation were approved by the Second Continental Congress in November 1777, which allowed for the states to maintain their militias yet did not state that the people individually had the right to keep and bear firearms.

Developments between 1777 and 1788

By 1788, Delaware, Pennsylvania, New Jersey, Georgia, and Connecticut had ratified the proposed second U.S. Constitution without any provision or right for people to own and bear firearms.

The Constitution was approved by nine states by June 1788 and was finally ratified on May 29, 1790. The First Congress met in March 1789 without a Bill of Rights or Second Amendment as part of the Constitution. Congress did not meet again until 1791.

In 1776, James Madison was involved in writing the final version of amendments to the Virginia state Constitution. He then served as a representative from Virginia to the Constitutional Convention of 1787. He was not only a representative but also a major contributor to the writing of the Constitution in 1787.

After losing the election to be a U.S. senator from Virginia, he was elected to be a member of the House of Representatives in 1789.

George Washington had no experience writing documents and speeches to give to Congress and began receiving advice on setting up the government, as well as assistance from "the Father of the Constitution" and his fellow Virginian, James Madison. Madison informed Washington that he wanted to propose amendments to the Constitution, based somewhat on the Virginia Declaration of Rights of 1776.

Washington approved of the idea of a Bill of Rights. In his inaugural address on April 30, 1789, Washington did not speak specifically about the Bill of Rights proposal.

According to author Richard Labunski's book, James Madison and the Struggle for the Bill of Rights, "Madison expected that Washington's endorsement would start the drive to win approval for constitutional amendments. Madison said (to House members) that the House should respect the decision of the Virginia General Assembly to request a second convention, but that any action should be consistent with the requirements of the Constitution. When two-thirds of the states requested such a gathering, Congress was bound to call one."

"On May 4, 1789, shortly after the legislative session of Congress had begun, Madison gave his colleagues notice that on the fourth Monday of the months to come, he would introduce proposed amendments to the Constitution."

He finally introduced his proposed amendments on June 8, 1789. Congress passed what became known as the Bill of Rights on September 25, 1789, and sent it to the states for ratification. When three-fourths of the states had ratified the Bill of Rights, Congress officially added it to the Constitution on December 15, 1791. The Second Amendment was now law in the United States.

It wasn't until 1939 that Massachusetts, Connecticut, and Georgia finally ratified the Bill of Rights. To this day, five state constitutions do not include the right to bear arms. They are California, Minnesota, New Jersey, New York, and Maryland.

It was not until 1875 that a Second Amendment case came before the Supreme Court. In 1875, in the case of Cruikshank v. United States, the Court decided to allow states to pass legislation regarding firearms.

Changes in the firearms industry from roughly 1776 to 1875

In the book The Gunning of America, authored by Pamela Haag, it states.

    A. "In the 1790s … the U.S. had a gun problem … it did not have enough of them. It had been undergunned in the Revolutionary War (and the country was still that way)."
    B. "No two guns were alike; the gunsmithing craft held. Some guns were bought in Europe."
    C. "Congress went to work, establishing the Springfield Armory to produce a good and efficient magazine."
    D. "In this time (around 1810 and on), the commercial success of Winchester, Colt, and others was largely the war business."
    E. "In 1849, Colt trailblazed the path that other gun industrialists; Remington, Smith & Wesson, and Winchester, would follow; they went abroad to sell their guns."

F. "The Civil War saved many gun manufacturers from extinction."

Also, in 1776, General Washington ordered the creation of an armory in Springfield, Massachusetts, first to store ammunition and guns, and later, as president, in 1790, guns began to be manufactured there. Later that decade, Congress funded the creation of the Harpers Ferry Armory in West Virginia to do the same.

Manufacturers and inventions from 1776 through the 1800s

A. Flintlock and long rifles were made by gunsmiths and by the government in armories, as well as by Remington.
B. Derringer, made by the Henry Deringer Company.
C. Colt .45 revolver, made by Colt and later by Smith & Wesson.
D. Shotguns, invented in England, made by Colt.
E. Gatling gun, invented by Richard Gatling and manufactured by Colt.

A. How were these weapons used to affect the culture and stability of the United States after the Bill of Rights, including the Second Amendment, became part of the Constitution, and who enforced laws throughout the nineteenth century?A. The country had to endure two major wars: the War of 1812 with the British and the Civil War. It also had other military conflicts with Mexico and Spain.

B. It is impossible to know how many Native Americans, also called Indigenous Americans, were killed with firearms during this time. It has been estimated that there were upwards of five million Native Americans living in what is now North America in the early 1600s, when Europeans began to arrive. With biological warfare, the taking of their lands, westward movement, and mass genocide carried out with guns, their population at the end of the nineteenth century was roughly 238,000 in North America.

C. In the so-called "Wild West," many crimes, such as train robberies, bank robberies, cattle rustling, shootouts, and cold-blooded murder, took place, with guns used to accomplish these crimes.

D. Animals were also victims of the use of guns during this time. Buffalo, also called bison, were slaughtered by the thousands. People like Buffalo Bill Cody killed an estimated 4,000 bison, and, of course, Native Americans also killed many, though often by methods other than guns.

E. With the westward movement following the Louisiana Purchase, President Jefferson's Lewis and Clark expedition confronted bears, and bears began to be killed with guns. Throughout the nineteenth century, the grizzly bear population was diminished substantially by hunters and alterations to their living conditions.

Law enforcement agencies used firearms for crime prevention and the enforcement of laws.

The U.S. Marshals Service was established in 1789 in the Judiciary Act.

A. Then there were sheriffs, a title that came from England. The first sheriffs on U.S. soil appeared in 1534, and they became the law enforcement officers of counties.

B. The most local law enforcement agency, found in cities and called the police, was founded in Boston in 1838.

How did the Supreme Court enforce the Second amendment

Article III of the U.S. Constitution establishes the court system, with the Supreme Court given the highest authority. There is no mention in the U.S. Constitution that allows the courts, including the Supreme Court, to amend or alter the articles of the Constitution or any amendment in the Bill of Rights. However, in the cases listed below, one can see that this is what some Supreme Court rulings did in cases involving the Second Amendment, according to Wikipedia.

In 1875, in a case named *United States v. Cruikshank*, part of the ruling of the justices, regarding the First and Second Amendments, stated that they "were not intended to limit the powers of the State governments in respect to their own citizens" and "have no other effect than to restrict the powers of the national government." The ruling allowed states to prosecute or protect people or organizations within their state for violating the Second Amendment, rather than the federal court system. The states were to protect their citizens' Second Amendment rights from the federal government, including Congress. This decision was an infringement, which is prohibited in the Second Amendment, if the state has control over the Second Amendment and not the U.S. Constitution.

In 1886, in *Presser v. Illinois*, part of the ruling of the nine justices who voted for it addressed "the rights of militia and individual[s]." The Court ruled that the Second Amendment right was a right of individuals, not militias, and was not a right to form or belong to a militia, but related to an individual's right to bear arms for the good of the United States. Nine men thus outvoted the legislators in the nine states that ratified the Second Amendment and the majority who voted for it in Congress and signed it into law under Washington in 1791.

In 1870, Congress created the Justice Department, adding another layer of law enforcement, specifically for criminal prosecutions.

Besides the courts interpreting the Second Amendment and law enforcement enforcing gun laws, the U.S. Senate has had a major role in determining who serves as the courts' decision-makers. According to the U.S. Constitution, Article II, section 2, the president of the United States nominates judges, and the U.S. Senate appoints and confirms those nominations. Thus, these two branches of government determine who serves on the courts. It was not until 1967 that someone other than a white man was seated on the bench of the Supreme Court: Thurgood Marshall. It was not until 1981 that a woman was seated on the bench of the Supreme Court: Sandra Day O'Connor.

In Article I, section 3 of the U.S. Constitution, each state is allotted two U.S. senators, each serving six-year terms. This structure gave more power to the least populated states and greater influence in approving judges and making laws relating to unlawful uses of firearms. This undemocratic, disproportional system has been responsible for many of the aforementioned decisions the Supreme Court has made in interpreting what the Second Amendment's authors, Madison and the other framers, intended by its language.

Federal and state gun control laws and regulations passed by Congress or state legislatures in the 1800s did not include any federal gun control laws or regulations that challenged the Second Amendment.

A few state legislatures passed laws restricting the use of guns that were challenged as violating Second Amendment rights, such as the state of Georgia, which in 1870 passed restrictions on carrying handguns, including pistols and revolvers, in public.

The Supreme Court in the state ruled against that law.

It's astounding that no federal gun control laws were passed despite all the mayhem, chaos, wars, crime, and insecurity on the streets in the United States, and that none of the first twenty-five presidents or fifty-five congressional sessions were involved. They must have fully embraced the amendment.

20th Century: Firearms, Manufacturers, and New Models

Wikipedia's "List of 20th-Century Weapons" includes the following.

Sidearms: Twenty-five, including Luger, Beretta 92 and 92R, M1911, Glock 17, and Browning Hi-Power. Their manufacturers include Colt, Browning, Remington, and Glock.

Submachine guns: Twenty types and brands, including the Thompson "Tommy Gun" (1920), Bergmann 34, Germany's Schmeisser 28, and Italy's Beretta 28.

Semiautomatic rifles: More than fifty, including the AR-15, Smith & Wesson, Wildcat made by Winchester, carbine made by Ruger, and the AK-47 by Kalashnikov.

Ammunition used in the above firearms in the 20th century

The most lethal and destructive ammunition involves clips and magazines for repeating rifles, which can hold up to fifty bullets. The first magazine was invented in Austria for its army in 1779. The Henry repeating firearm was invented in 1860 in the United States and was used by the North in the Civil War. The first semiautomatic pistol was invented in 1893 and was named the Borchardt C-93. Since then, two of the best-known semiautomatic rifles that use magazines are the Ruger 10/22 and the AR-15 in the United States.

Bullets were made more harmful to the human body during the twentieth century. One of the better-known types is the jacketed hollow point, in which the bullet expands once inside the body and causes much more damage. Another type of ammunition that causes greater harm is known as +P ammo, in which the bullet's speed is increased substantially before entering the body.

How were these new types and models of firearms, bullets, and magazines used in the United States in the twentieth century?

What has been called "organized crime," beginning in the 1920s following the passage of the Eighteenth Amendment to the Bill of Rights, which restricted the sale and consumption of liquor, led to many homicides, with Al Capone's and "Bugs" Moran's gangs clashing. By 1926, there were at least 12,000 homicides yearly in the United States. Bank robberies continued, especially during the "Public Enemy" era of the 1930s. Bonnie and Clyde, Pretty Boy Floyd, and John Dillinger were some of the better-known bank robbers.

With two world wars involving U.S. participation in the first half of the twentieth century, many people around the world were victims of firearms use. Approximately eighty million people were killed in those two wars.

Street gangs are another source of deadly gun violence. They began to appear in the United States as early as 1783, before the Second Amendment became law in 1791. Of course, those gangs were in East Coast states. They came west to Chicago with Al Capone in the Roaring Twenties. They have spread since then across the United States, with an estimated 20,000 gangs and as many as one million gang members. Their purposes and tactics have changed over the centuries. Gang members are responsible for as many as 2,000 homicides in the United States in recent years.

Bank and Brinks robberies occurred throughout the twentieth century. Even though firearms were used in thousands of these robberies, less than one percent led to death. The greatest number of robberies took place in 1991, when there were 9,388; that number has declined since then.

Kidnapping was widely reported in 1932 with the abduction of Charles Lindbergh's baby daughter. However, that crime was reported as early as 1874. Guns have been used in this crime.

Mass shootings began in 1920, when at least thirty Black voters were killed in the Ocoee, Florida, massacre. Another notable mass shooting took place in 1966 from a tower at the University of Texas. An M1 carbine, along with a sawed-off shotgun, was used to kill fourteen people and wound as many as thirty-three. Incidents of mass shootings continued throughout the twentieth century, ending with the April 20, 1999, Columbine High School shooting.

In Colorado, a mass shooting left twelve students and one teacher dead, and twenty-one others were injured. The killers used several weapons, including a modified hunting rifle and a sawed-off shotgun. The two teenage boys who committed this crime killed themselves with their own guns.

Hate homicides with guns have been based on biases relating to race, ethnicity, religion, sexual orientation, and political ideology. There were also hate-motivated mass shootings in the twentieth century, such as the one in Rosewood, Florida, in 1923, where Black people were shot. Medgar Evers was killed for his participation in the civil rights movement in 1963, along with the assassination of Dr. Martin Luther King Jr. in 1968.

In 1973, the term "domestic violence" began to be used. Women sought legal protections from abuse, physical harm, and even being shot to death by their husbands or boyfriends. Statistically, if there is a gun in the family home, women face a greater risk of becoming victims. Guns are used to threaten, coerce, control, or kill.

Serial killers in the twentieth century numbered about 750 and killed an estimated 5,300 to 6,300 people in the United States. Some of the more notable serial killers who shot their victims were the Zodiac Killer and David Richard Berkowitz, also known as the "Son of Sam," who was involved in at least eight shootings.

There were numerous other ways and reasons people were killed with guns in the United States during the twentieth century, including road rage, cartels selling and transporting drugs and guns, accidental shootings in the home by children finding their parents' guns due to improper storage, crimes committed with guns such as robberies, home intrusions, and carjackings, and even mistakes such as police shooting innocent suspects. Suicide by gun is more prevalent in the United States than in any other country.

<u>Federal and state laws enacted in the twentieth century as a result of deaths due to gun use in the United States</u>

Unlike the nineteenth century, when few gun control laws were passed, both federal and state legislatures enacted laws in the twentieth century, which presidents and governors signed. Below is a sample of some significant ones:

Federal Law

- 1934 National Firearms Act: The first federal law banning the manufacture, sale, or possession of automatic guns such as submachine guns, sawed-off shotguns, and silencers.
- 1938 Federal Firearms Act: Required manufacturers, importers of guns, and businesses selling firearms to obtain licenses to do business in the United States.
- 1968 Gun Control Act: Further regulated the firearms industry and firearms ownership.

- 1988 Undetectable Firearms Act: Prohibits the manufacture, importation, sale, or possession of firearms that are undetectable by walk-through metal detector devices.
- 1994 Violent Crime Control and Law Enforcement Act: Banned assault weapons, including AR-15s, AK-47s, and other types of assault firearms, from being manufactured, imported, or sold in the United States. It had a ten-year term.

State Laws

- In the early 1900s, across the country, up to forty-three states had some form of gun control laws or regulations on the books. Some laws restricted carrying guns in public, while others imposed requirements for owning a firearm. The NRA at the time was not actively involved in curbing legislation.
- 1967: The California legislature passed, and the governor signed, the Mulford Act in response to Black Panther group members carrying loaded firearms into the State Capitol building. The law prohibits carrying a loaded firearm in public or in a car in protected areas of the state.
- 1976: The District of Columbia passed a law banning handguns and requiring the registration of all guns.
- 1989: California passed a law banning the ownership and sale of various semiautomatic firearms.
- 1998: The state of Massachusetts passed a law requiring gun purchasers to obtain a license from the gun dealer selling them a gun.

<u>How Gun Rights Lobbyist Groups and Advocates for Gun Safety, Restrictions, or Controls Have Influenced the Enactment of State and Federal Legislation</u>

The most notable organization that has been effective in influencing legislators, politicians, the courts, and the public during the twentieth century is the National Rifle Association

(NRA). Having its inception purpose to help train individuals to become better at shooting weapons in the nineteenth century following the Civil War, it began to address gun safety, restrictions, and control laws more frequently as the twentieth century unfolded.

Following the Civil War and the assassination of President Lincoln, people became more cognizant of the power of guns in affecting society and personal protection. The NRA had its birth in the early 1870s, and within a few years President James Garfield was assassinated, followed by the assassination of President William McKinley in 1901—all three presidents having been killed by gunshots. During this period, the United States was also engaged in another war, the Spanish-American War.

For quite a few years, as the NRA's membership grew, it became more involved in forming opinions regarding gun laws. It contributed to writing legislation and cooperated in its enactment. For instance, the NRA worked with Congress and President Roosevelt to pass the 1934 National Firearms Act and the 1938 Federal Firearms Act.

However, with the assassination of President John F. Kennedy in 1963, the mass shooting at the University of Texas in 1966, and the shootings of civil rights champion Dr. Martin Luther King Jr. and presidential candidate Robert F. Kennedy in the first half of 1968, along with the massive unrest in the country due to U.S. involvement in the Vietnam War, Congress created the Consumer Product Safety Act in 1972.

The NRA challenged an amendment to the act that would have included guns on the product list. The organization was no longer supportive of efforts to protect Americans against the risks of guns, and by 1975, the NRA had created its first lobbying subdivision, called the Institute for Legislative Action.

In 1980, the NRA endorsed Ronald Reagan for president. Even though he had signed a gun control bill in the 1960s as governor of California, he was now opposed to strong gun restrictions and controls.

He was shot very early in his tenure, along with his press secretary, Jim Brady. He and his wife, Sarah, later created the Brady Campaign to Prevent Gun Violence.

The Brady Campaign got to work and helped Congress pass the Brady Handgun Violence Prevention Act in 1993, which required a waiting period between the purchase and delivery of handguns. The country now had an effective organization that could somewhat offset the lobbying power of the NRA.

As with each century, there is the introduction of new kinds of firearms, followed by crimes using those firearms. State or federal legislators then create new laws, and finally, groups such as the NRA in the twentieth century have sought to have the courts rule against those laws. Here are some examples.

<u>Supreme Court, Federal, and State Rulings on Cases Brought Against These and Other Laws Regarding Second Amendment Rights</u>

With the assassination of three U.S. presidents in the nineteenth century and increased criminal behavior involving more deadly weapons in the early twentieth century, the courts might rein in what some believed to be absolute rights under the Second Amendment for citizens to own any type of firearm for self-protection.

In 1939, the Supreme Court overturned a U.S. district court ruling in *United States v. Miller.* The Court ruled that the Second Amendment does not permit a citizen to buy and own a double-barreled shotgun with an eighteen-inch barrel, thereby overruling the lower court.

Miller and his cohorts were transporting such a weapon from one state to another, making it an interstate matter, which became a key issue. According to the government's argument, only weapons used by a well-regulated militia and registered under the National Firearms Act of 1934 were deemed permissible for individual ownership, and the short-barreled shotgun was not among those weapons. The Supreme Court ruled that certain firearms are not protected under the Second Amendment and referred to both clauses of the amendment in its decision.

In 1968, Congress amended the NFA to expand the types of weapons and devices covered in the 1934 act to include items such as guns with a barrel bore larger than one-half inch in diameter, machine-gun frames, and conversion kits.

The National Firearms Act of 1934 has faced additional challenges over the years. In 1971, in the *United States v. Freed* Supreme Court decision, the Court ruled that the registration requirement in the NFA was within constitutional limits. Over the years, the courts have expanded, clarified, modified, and adopted various interpretations of the Second Amendment throughout the twentieth century.

The *Lewis v. United States* case is another example of the evolving understanding of the Second Amendment, along with other federal governmental acts and laws. In this Supreme Court ruling, after **many** attempts in lower courts, the Court ultimately ruled that a person legally convicted of a felony may not own or possess a firearm, thus adding an additional layer to the amendment.

Twenty-First Century: New Firearms, Manufacturers, and Ammunition

What are the most popular brands and firearms created since the beginning of this century? Of the 663 gun manufacturers in the United States in 2023, several dominate the market due to demand for their products, mostly pistols and revolvers.

The following accounted for approximately 15 percent of annual gun sales in recent years: the Ruger Blackhawk revolver, Smith & Wesson 9 pistol, Ruger Mark IV pistol, Marlin Model 1895 lever-action rifle, Ruger bolt-action rifle, and Ruger 10/22 semiautomatic rifle. Other manufacturers performing well include Glock, Colt, Browning, Magnum Research, Armscor, Sig Sauer, Beretta, and others.

There are many gun manufacturers around the world producing semiautomatic handguns, including Beretta, Glock, and Remington, as well as rifles by Ruger and Smith & Wesson.

According to a recent ATF report, the number of firearms manufactured in the United States has increased by 187 percent since the year 2000, and imports of firearms have risen by 359 percent.

Handguns have now been developed that can be converted into semiautomatic firearms. They are very popular. Many are being converted into "ghost guns" by using conversion kits produced by 3D printers. These firearms are not traceable because they do not have serial numbers.

According to an NBC News national poll released in 2023, 52 percent of Americans reported that they or someone in their household possessed a firearm.

Crime and Use of New Types of Firearms and Ammunition

According to ATF data, more than one million guns were stolen from private citizens from 2017 to 2021. Many of these firearms were later used in the commission of crimes.

Ammunition **is** required to operate firearms and is measured by caliber, the size of a bullet. The calibers most frequently used in handgun homicides in the United States in recent years, from smallest to largest, are 9mm, .45 ACP, .38, .380 ACP, and .357 Magnum. The 9mm caliber is used most often in homicides.

These are not the most lethal caliber bullets one could use to ensure a fatal shooting. It has been suggested that shooters may be ignorant or impulsive when planning and carrying out their actions.

Another aspect of homicide, according to studies, is the location where the victim is struck by a bullet and whether that location is likely to be fatal. The chest is the most common location, accounting for about 75 percent of fatal shootings; approximately 55 percent of victims die if shot in the abdomen, and 53 percent if shot in the head.

What these different calibers and types of bullets do to the human body upon entry varies significantly. According to the Gun Caliber Statistics report of 2024, one in six people shot with a firearm dies. In an article titled "What a Bullet Does to the Human Body," it was reported that "there is a tremendous difference in the amount of energy associated with a bullet from an AR-15 rifle and that of a handgun." Smock stated, "With a rifle round wound, you have a massive disruption. Rather than three-quarters of an inch around the wound path, the tissue is disrupted three to four inches around the same area."

Expanding bullets have been around for many years, but they are now much more damaging. According to the Wikipedia article titled "Expanding Bullet," these bullets are known colloquially as dum-dum bullets. Two common designs are the hollow-point and soft-point bullet. These and other expanding bullets are intended to expand upon impact with a human body and to expand quickly to cause the greatest possible wounding or death to the target. Militaries around the world that observe the Hague Convention have agreed not to use them.

Homicides are the most notable and impactful crimes committed using firearms. In 2019, the Centers for Disease Control reported that 19,141 homicides occurred in the United States. Handguns are used more than 60 percent of the time. Only Mexico, Turkey, and Estonia have higher homicide rates per 100,000 population than the United States.

Gang violence resulting in homicides represents the largest segment of all homicides, accounting for about 13 percent annually, according to the National Youth Gang Survey Analysis. There have been an estimated 27,000 to 30,000 gangs nationwide in recent years, with approximately 770,000 to 850,000 members. The larger gangs are located in major cities such as Los Angeles and Chicago, but gangs are also present in suburban and rural areas. In a separate study, it was estimated that 92 percent of gang members were male and 8 percent female. The 2002 VC Archives also reported that gang membership by race was estimated as follows: Latino, 46 percent; African American, 34 percent; Caucasian, 12 percent; Asian, 6 percent; and other, 2 percent. In one survey, half of gang members reported owning a gun. Most homicide incidents occur in large cities and involve young males.

Mass shootings are another form of gun violence. According to a Wikipedia article, "no broad definition exists"; however, Mother Jones magazine has adopted the definition of a mass shooting as one in which "a gunman kills at least four people in a public place, excluding gang-related shootings." Mass shootings have increased in number in the United States, which experiences more of them than all other developed countries. There were twelve mass shootings in 2023. The AR-15–style rifle has been the weapon of choice in approximately 26 percent of mass shootings, although handguns remain the most commonly used weapon.

Robberies and carjackings continue to be crimes facilitated by firearms. However, the rate of robberies has been decreasing since the 1990s, when there were almost 700,000 per year. In 2022, there were just over 200,000. Criminals need to intimidate victims, so a firearm is often used. The most readily available firearm is typically a handgun. Individuals must remain alert to where they park their cars and be cautious when someone attempts to gain access to a vehicle using a staged or phony accident. Not keeping large amounts of cash in registers and securing expensive items in locked display cases may help reduce risk. Most smash-and-grab criminals do not use guns.

Domestic violence homicides involving firearms are an extremely serious and growing category of gun-related crime in the United States. According to a comprehensive analysis by EFSGV, 91.6 percent of women killed by guns in high-income countries in 2019 were killed in the United States. The report further states, "Around 4.5 million women in the U.S. have been threatened with a gun, and nearly one million have been shot or shot at by an intimate partner." Additionally, "77.4 percent of victims of intimate partner homicides are women," and "women are five times more likely to be murdered by an abusive partner when the abuser has access to a gun." Federal law prohibits the purchase and possession of firearms by individuals convicted of misdemeanor crimes of domestic violence; however, not all states adhere to or consistently enforce this law. Federal law also does not require the removal of firearms already possessed by abusers at the time they become prohibited. The type of firearm used in domestic violence shootings depends on the firearms owned or possessed by the abuser at the time of the incident.

Home invasions and burglaries involving a firearm are another serious category of crime and can result in the deaths of household members. According to a Bureau of Justice Statistics special report from September 2010, an average of 3.7 million household burglaries occurred each year from 2003 to 2007.

In about 28 percent of those burglaries, a household member was present during the incident. Thirty percent of individuals experiencing violence during a completed burglary faced an armed offender, and 23 percent of those armed offenders had firearms. An average of 430 burglary-related homicides occurred annually. According to another source, there is no single type of firearm used by criminals; it may be a handgun, a shotgun, or even an AR-15–style firearm.

Children finding and discharging firearms in the **home** has caused the deaths of both themselves and other children. According to the National Violent Death Reporting System (U.S.), 2003–2021, "Unintentional injury is a leading cause of death among U.S. children and adolescents aged 0–17, and firearms are a leading injury mechanism." If a parent owns a firearm while children are living in the household, the parent must take all possible preventive measures, including locking up the firearm, unloading it, and storing ammunition in a separate, locked location. Self-inflicted injuries account for 37.8 percent of firearm-related injuries and deaths. "During 2002–2021, a total of 1,262 fatal unintentional firearm injury cases among children aged 0–17 were identified." How many cases were not identified remains unknown.

Obviously, not all types of shootings are listed here, but the public has asked, demanded, and lobbied for state and federal legislators to address this unacceptable level of firearm violence.

<u>Gun Control Laws Passed by State and Federal Governments in the Twenty-First Century in the United States</u>

In September 2004, Congress allowed the 1994 Violent Crime Control and Law Enforcement Act to expire after its ten-year term, which had included a ban on assault firearms such as the AR-15.

The Protection of Lawful Commerce in Arms Act was signed in October 2005, giving gun manufacturers and gun dealers protections that limited a plaintiff's ability to sue them for liability.

In February 2012, the National Parks Gun Act allowed licensed gun owners to enter national parks with their firearms for hunting, provided they were not violating any state laws prohibiting such activity. This law overturned a twenty-year ban on bringing loaded guns into national parks.

Congress approved the *Sportsmen's* Heritage and Recreational Enhancement Act in 2017–18, declaring that federal land must be open to hunting and recreational shooting, subject to certain procedures and protocols.

In 2020, the U.S. Department of Justice imposed a ban on bump stocks, which could be attached to semiautomatic firearms to enable automatic firing. Owners of firearms equipped with bump stocks were required to dispose of them. This requirement has since been overturned.

The Bipartisan Safer Communities Act was passed and signed into law in 2022. The law provides funding for states to establish crisis intervention programs and supports the implementation of red flag policies and mental health assistance.

Supreme Court and State Court Rulings in the Twenty-First Century, Along with Congressional Actions on Gun Control Laws

In 2004, Congress did not extend the 1994 Violent Crime Control and Law Enforcement Act when it reached the end of its ten-year term. As a result, nineteen different types of military-style assault firearms were no longer prohibited from being sold in the United States.

In June 2008, the Supreme Court of the United States ruled on a case titled District of Columbia v. Heller. Heller was a resident of Washington, D.C., who sought to have the Court overturn lower court rulings that allowed the District to enforce the Firearms Control Regulations Act of 1975. The district court had granted a motion to dismiss the challenge to the law.

In its 2008 decision, the Supreme Court based its ruling on a new interpretation. The Court rejected the framers' binding of the two clauses of the Second Amendment that linked militia service to the right of the people to keep and bear arms. The justice who authored the majority opinion emphasized an individual right by interpreting the plural noun "people" in the second clause as conferring an individual right, thereby rejecting the previous "collective rights" theory that centered on state militias. This decision departed from traditional constitutional interpretations of the Second Amendment grounded in stare decisis and earlier Supreme Court rulings. The ruling ultimately allowed significantly greater freedom for individuals to purchase and possess firearms.

New York State Rifle & Pistol Association, Inc. v. Bruen (2022): This case was filed after two individuals were denied licenses to carry firearms in public for self-protection. The state of New York had a number of gun safety regulations and requirements in place, including mandatory training, licensing, mental health evaluations, and a demonstrated need to carry a firearm in public. The U.S. Supreme Court decided in favor of the two individuals, relying on the 2008 District of Columbia v. Heller ruling as a basis. The Court stated that New York could not use a "may issue" standard for issuing licenses but must instead apply a "shall issue" standard.

Garland v. Cargill (2024): The Supreme Court overturned a federal government ban on bump stock devices. Following a 2017 executive order issued after the Las Vegas shooting, which killed 58 people and injured hundreds more, the Bureau of Alcohol, Tobacco, Firearms and Explosives (ATF) analyzed bump stocks and their operational function. The agency determined that bump stocks fell within the definition of machine guns, which are banned under the National Firearms Act of 1934.

Summary of Historical Phases

This examination of the invention of firearms, their continued development, and their consequences for humanity can be understood in several phases. The invention, development, and manufacture of firearms constitute phase one. The use of firearms, including crime and punishment, represents phase two. Phase three encompasses reactions to phase two and includes politics, laws, and regulations. Phase four involves interpretations and challenges to phase three, including court decisions and the continuation of these phases, resulting in an unacceptable number of human lives lost.

Some Possible Solutions to Significantly Change the Dynamics of These Four Phases of America's Violent Gun Culture

A. Take action regarding the courts' interpretation of the Second Amendment following the *Heller* decision.

B. Amend the amendment using Justice John Paul Stevens's suggestion: "People can keep and bear arms when serving in the real militia.

C. Repeal or amend the Second Amendment through the adoption of a new Twenty-Eighth Amendment.

There had been a somewhat traditional historical understanding within the court system regarding the Second Amendment until it was drastically modified by the Supreme Court in its 2008 District of Columbia v. Heller decision. The Court largely did not consider the first clause relating to a "well-regulated militia" and instead focused almost entirely on the second clause relating to the right of the people to keep and bear arms. The current Supreme Court could revisit the Second Amendment and consider that the militia may now be understood as a state's National Guard.

From the article titled "Repeal the Second Amendment: The Case for a Safer America," written by Alan J. Lichtman:

"As a panel of linguists and professors of English stated in an amicus brief submitted in the *Heller* case, people at the time would not have read the Second Amendment as protecting an individual's right to bear arms independent of militias. Authorities on early American usage demonstrate that the term 'bear arms' is an idiomatic expression meaning 'to serve as a soldier.'"

Another possible solution would be to change the makeup of the Supreme Court to create a majority that would interpret the Second Amendment as the framers intended.

D. Reamend the Second Amendment through a new amendment, similar to what occurred with the Eighteenth and Twenty-First Amendments. For example:

Twenty-Eighth Amendment: This amendment hereby amends and replaces the Second Amendment. The nation's military branches and state military organizations, such as the National Guard, shall be responsible for protecting the nation and state property. Firearm laws shall be enforced by all law enforcement agencies authorized to do so. An individual's right to purchase and own a firearm for protection or other activities shall be subject to federal and state violence prevention and public safety laws.

CHAPTER TWENTY

Roberto has now submitted his segment. It has been nearly two months. The group was brought back together when he resumed the Zoom session on a Monday at 2:00 p.m. PST.

KO: I can see you, Clyde, but I can't hear you. Roberto put a hand up to his ear to indicate the issue.

PM: Congratulations, Roberto! Now I can completely understand why you were an academic scholar.

SW: Thanks for resuming our communication. It's been a while, and many things have transpired. However, you've spent your time being an architect. The structure of your segment is well laid out and very informative.

Rx: Are you guys trying to mute me? KO, you sure took a long time, and you are too loquacious. Who in their right mind is going to muddle through your multitude of factoids? Don't expect such a long, wordy segment from me.

YY: Wow! I feel like I did in school reading highly cerebral material. I had heard about the Chinese and gunpowder, but I didn't know that my ancestors had anything to do with developing firearms back then.

ET: Hi, everyone! It's good to see your handsome faces again. I want to commend you, Roberto, for producing an A-plus term paper, I mean, segment. There is so much information presented, dating back to England and the early days of our country, especially Virginia.

KO: Clyde, I realize there are many facts and much information in my segment. I was trying to provide as much detail as I could. Emily, thank you for your kind words. Yes, Virginia, especially Jamestown, has played a major role in shaping the gun culture in our country.

ET: By the way, have you all become aware that the surgeon general of the United States has declared the gun violence problem to be a public health emergency?

Rx: That political appointee is just mouthing what his boss in the White House wants him to declare.

PM: That declaration is very important to what we are dealing with. The SG is acknowledging what we all know, that in many parts of our country, one can't walk down the street safely, children can't be in school 100 percent safely, and women are much more vulnerable to being shot when there is a severe gun violence problem.

ET: I agree with you, Mark. Roberto, thanks for laying the foundation for our firearms problems. It is the manufacturers who keep developing more powerful, destructive firearms who should share much of the blame for the gun violence we have in our country.

ET: What's good about this surgeon general advisory is that it will provide funding for research, mental health assistance, and other valuable resources for preventing this crisis.

Rx: KO, you sure think highly of yourself. It's one thing to provide a historical list of subsets of firearms development over the centuries, but it's quite another to think you are capable of amending one of the most cherished amendments in our Bill of Rights. Have you been diagnosed as narcissistic?

YY: Roberto, you have provided us with plenty of food for thought. Now, can the rest of us make equal contributions to our resolution to create powerful suggestions to ameliorate the extreme gun violence problem in our country?

ET: Clyde, shame on you! Roberto has obviously put a lot of effort and thought into creating his segment. I can tell you from my counseling experience that he is not a narcissistic person. We need bold proposals such as the ones he has produced.

PM: I agree with Roberto that the Second Amendment needs to be rewritten so that the average person can read and understand it without requiring a judge to interpret it for clarification. If it is acceptable to all of you, I will be submitting my segment next. I have been working on it, as most of you have been working on yours.

SW: Thanks, Mark, for volunteering to create and submit the next segment. Unless Emily wishes to go next, I support you being next in line. Roberto has given us a fabulous segment, and hopefully we can match his effort as we meet the challenge we have undertaken.

ET: Thanks, Shahzad, for thinking of me. However, I think Mark's segment dealing with law enforcement responsibilities, the laws to enforce, criminal gangs with guns, recidivism, and related issues is a good follow-up to Roberto's segment. Go for it!

KO: Thanks, Mark. I figured you would step up to the plate next. Your segment seems to be the most logical one to follow mine, since you will be dealing with gun-related crime more than the others. I have collected many articles, research materials, and other resources that I haven't used.

If you think I may have information you can use, just let me know. Best wishes in creating a very formidable segment that will influence readers to join us.

YY: Good luck, Mark! I have confidence in your ability and knowledge to create a segment that covers your area of expertise. I'll be eagerly awaiting what you submit.

Rx: Okay, let's see what a rookie cop can produce. Just keep it shorter than KO's presentation.

PM: Thanks, all. See you later.

MARK JACKSON'S SEGMENT

Enforcement of laws passed by the many legislative bodies and agencies in our country is massive and requires an enormous amount of training, skill, effort, and responsibility to carry out. Legislation pertaining to the Second Amendment requires special implementation. What follows is a brief history of law enforcement in the United States and the specific issues law enforcement must address regarding gun control laws and crimes involving firearms.

Let us first examine the history of policing in the country. Having individuals on the streets who can provide security for citizens, whether in public spaces or in their homes, day or night, has long been considered valuable. In the English-founded colonies, England's methods of policing were continued. According to the article "Early Police in the United States," written by Jean-Paul Brodeur and Michael Parker Banton, English policing culture, along with Anglo-Saxon common law and norms, was brought to the colonies.

One of the earliest forms of policing was called the Night Watch system, described in the article "A Brief History of Policing in the United States." The system "required all able-bodied males to donate their time to protect the cities." In the early 1700s, a "day watch system" was established in larger colonial cities.

Like the English, Americans were "wary of creating standing police forces." However, in 1631, a police force was established in Boston, followed by one in New York City in 1647.

By 1658, police began to be paid. In the Carolinas, police were organized into patrols in 1704 to prevent slave rebellions.

The article "Early Police in the United States" also discusses civilian reformers in major cities such as New York and Boston who struggled to improve policing in immigrant communities and bring greater political control over police forces. Requirements for uniforms and rules of behavior were established.

Boston established a full-time police force in 1838.

In 1844, police officers in New York began being paid by the city for their service. Their main objectives were to control gambling, prostitution, and civil unrest.

For a period during the eighteenth and early nineteenth centuries, vigilante groups attempted to enforce laws and administer justice in some areas. During this time, it was difficult to persuade communities to establish formal police departments.

The passage of the Second Amendment in 1791 marked a shift in thinking, attitudes, and political decision-making.

During this era, around 1783, some early forms of street gangs emerged, according to the *National* Gang Center Bulletin (May 2010). "Gang emergence in the Northeast and Midwest was fueled by immigration and poverty. The earliest gangs of New York were not criminal." The report further states that "more dangerous street gangs than previously seen emerged around 1820." There was widespread poverty, the growth of slum neighborhoods, unemployment, and desperation in major cities.

With the passage of the Naturalization Act in 1790, Congress addressed issues of citizenship relatively quickly. "The law enabled those who had resided in the country for two years and had lived in their current state of residence for one year to apply for citizenship."

With the Second Amendment's passage in 1791 and President Washington's approval, law enforcement assumed a more defined rationale for owning and bearing firearms. Males were expected to offer their service to a militia.

Supreme Court decisions since that time have significantly changed the original intention of that amendment.

Frank Jastrzembski, in his article "The History of Gun Control in the United States, Part 2," states, "Gun control in the nineteenth century in America was more restrictive than in previous centuries. During this period, states implemented laws that imposed greater restrictions on carrying firearms and introduced regulations against concealed weapons."

In the South, firearms were used extensively when the Civil War broke out on April 12, 1861. During the Civil War, the military became the primary form of authority in the Southern states, and law enforcement in those states took on an even greater challenge.

In the 1870s, following London, England's lead, law enforcement departments in major cities began establishing investigative units and training officers to become "detectives."

The demographics of large cities in the East changed substantially with immigration from Germany and Italy. Americans of English and Dutch heritage who had settled earlier saw their social dominance eroded. Crime and rioting increased, and political decision-makers had to adjust policies for inclusion.

During this era, around 1783, early forms of street gangs emerged, according to the National Gang Center Bulletin (May 2010). "Gang emergence in the Northeast and Midwest was fueled by immigration and poverty. The earliest gangs of New York were not criminal." The report further states that "more dangerous street gangs than previously seen emerged around 1820." There was widespread poverty, slum neighborhoods, unemployment, and desperation in major cities.

Policing methods evolved significantly in many ways from the beginning of law enforcement in our country.

Over the nineteenth and early twentieth centuries, law enforcement changed in numerous ways. Some departments in the East began using a particular model of policing. Uniforms were introduced, and formal training became required. As each city established its own police department, police stationing became decentralized.

In 1905, the first state police agency was created in Pennsylvania. According to Wikipedia, "The advent of the police two-way radio and telephone in the early twentieth century transformed policing into a reactive strategy, responding to calls for service."

From the beginning of policing in the United States, various means of transportation were available to officers. Initially, officers traveled on foot and horseback. Horses and buggies, as well as boats, later became available. In the nineteenth century, a major innovation—the railroad—allowed police to travel much greater distances in shorter periods of time. Then, in the 1890s, the automobile became available, creating a significant change. Early automobiles were electrically charged vehicles capable of traveling approximately thirty miles before requiring recharging.

Regarding police communication between departments and agencies, early systems began in 1633 in Massachusetts with the

U.S. Mail service. By 1860, the telegraph allowed communication across the country between the East and West Coasts.

Communication technology was significantly enhanced by 1892, when Alexander Graham Bell's telephone allowed people to make long-distance calls.

Following the introduction of the electric wagon police vehicle, Ford, General Motors, and Chrysler began producing gasoline-powered cars that police departments adopted. This led to the invention of a new technology in the early twentieth century: the police car equipped with two-way radios.

Not only did transportation and communication technologies change significantly, but firearms did as well. From the early days of America, when flintlock rifles and pistols were common, there was a transformative shift by the twentieth century to firearms such as semiautomatic pistols and machine guns capable of rapid fire, discharging multiple rounds with a single function of the trigger. It is remarkable that it was legal to purchase a machine gun in the United States a century ago.

These weapons and others were used in criminal activity during the Prohibition era of American history. Following figures such as Butch Cassidy and the Sundance Kid, law enforcement became increasingly dangerous as new types of criminals emerged who directly challenged police authority. Criminal gangs such as the Chicago Outfit, led by Al Capone, were responsible for the St. Valentine's Day Massacre in 1929, in which seven people were killed using two Thompson submachine guns.

It took nearly a year for federal law enforcement (G-men) to arrest just one of the killers.

Wikipedia's "St. Valentine's Day Massacre" article points out, "The perpetrators have never been conclusively identified. The killers opened fire with Thompson submachine guns, one with a 20-round box magazine and the other with a 50-round drum." A sheriff's department in Michigan became involved near the end of 1929 and was able to supply the name of the registered owner of the Cadillac used in the crime.

At one point, police used the new science of forensic ballistics to identify both weapons. This required extensive work by many individuals, including experts at the time, as well as cooperation among different law enforcement agencies and the use of new investigative tools to solve much of the crime. Al Capone was not indicted for the massacre.

Congress eventually moved to limit the sale and ownership of machine guns and submachine guns under the National Firearms Act of 1934. It was not until 1986 that Congress went further and banned the possession of those weapons in the United States.

The Supreme Court ultimately ruled against owning a machine gun or submachine gun in 1939 in a case titled United States v. Miller.

During the first half of the twentieth century, policing reform was significantly advanced by a man named August Vollmer. He was an innovator in policing concepts and advocated for higher education, including college degrees, for police officers. He introduced concepts from sociology, psychology, management, and technology into law enforcement.

He also pushed for accountability in policing practices, particularly those involving unconstitutional conduct and mental or physical abuse. He wanted police officers to be more civil and professional.

Public perception of police protection increased further following World War II. As the country emerged from the Great Depression and reduced military spending, it was able to invest more resources in crime prevention, including increased numbers of police cars patrolling streets and neighborhoods.

With this shift, law enforcement also had to begin addressing the expanding gang problem in the 1940s and the decades that followed. According to the Wikipedia article "Gangs in the United States," "gangs reemerged in the Northeast in cities such as New York during the second half of the twentieth century with rising Latin immigration, especially from Puerto Rico." As many Black Americans moved from Southern states to the Midwest, Black gangs began to emerge in the 1950s in Chicago. Police in Los Angeles also had to contend with Mexican gangs associated with increased immigration, as well as Black gangs. Law enforcement further faced resistance from white populations, including during events such as the Zoot Suit riots.

"Black gangs began forming territorial-based groups by the early 1970s." There was also violence involving Black organizations such as the Black Panthers. Motorcycle gangs, including the Hells Angels, became an additional concern. Drugs, gambling, and related crimes were the primary criminal activities of these gangs.

A different set of law enforcement challenges emerged in the 1960s with the rise of anti–Vietnam War protests.

The United States had been engaged in Vietnam since the late 1940s following the withdrawal of French forces. However, it was not until the 1960s that U.S. troops were stationed in South Vietnam in an effort to prevent the communist government of North Vietnam from controlling the entire country.

Among the many demonstrations in the United States against involvement in the Vietnam conflict, the Wikipedia article titled "List of Protests Against the Vietnam War" notes that Quakers, in 1960, "surrounded the Pentagon for part of two days" in a peaceful protest.

Police involvement in that protest was likely minimal. However, as U.S. involvement increased—from military advisors to the deployment of troops—protests expanded. In May 1964, hundreds of students protested in New York City and in front of the United Nations. Approximately 700 protesters marched in San Francisco, with smaller demonstrations occurring in Seattle and Wisconsin. Police were required to monitor protests around United Nations property and adjust to these evolving circumstances.

On June 23, 1967, "1,300 police attacked peace activists at the Century Plaza Hotel in Los Angeles," where the U.S. president was being honored.

In August 1968, the Democratic Party's convention was in turmoil. Outside the convention, between 7,000 and 10,000 protesters engaged in violent activity, and many were arrested and brought to trial, including several well-known leaders.

On May 4, 1969, at Kent State University in Ohio, National Guard troops stationed there to control a protest shot and killed four students who were not involved in violence of any kind. In 1970, two students were also shot and killed during a protest at Jackson State College in Mississippi.

In August 1970, a bombing targeted an Army Math Research Center but missed its intended target at the University of Wisconsin.

In March 1971, the Weathermen planted a bomb in the U.S. Capitol building, causing $300,000 in damage but no casualties.

In April 1972, 100,000 people marched in New York City, 12,000 in Los Angeles, and 25,000 in San Francisco.

Law enforcement agencies were kept very busy maintaining law and order across many locations over several years, continuing until the end of the war in 1975.

Not only did protesters sometimes become violent, but police misconduct also involved violence. During the Civil Rights Movement beginning in the 1950s, Rosa Parks and later Dr. Martin Luther King Jr. challenged racial bias. Racial prejudice often influenced police officers' responses to Black demonstrators in the South.

Dr. Martin Luther King Jr. was later assassinated in Memphis, Tennessee, with a high-velocity rifle bullet in April 1968. The shooter was positioned across the street at the time of the shooting.

In Southern states, such as during the John Lewis–led protest in 1965 on the Edmund Pettus Bridge in Alabama, demonstrators were confronted by local police who severely beat many of the approximately 6,000 participants. The event was later referred to as "Bloody Sunday." This incident was classified as police misconduct by the U.S. Department of Justice.

A more recent and serious example of police misconduct occurred in Minneapolis in 2020, when four police officers unnecessarily attempted to subdue George Floyd, a Black man. He was handcuffed, placed face down on the street pavement, and killed after an officer knelt on him for an extended period. The four officers were tried and convicted in state court, and the lead officer was also tried in federal court.

According to the Wikipedia article "Law Enforcement in the United States," "a 2021 study published in The Lancet found that 30,000 people died as a result of police violence in the U.S. from 1980 to 2018."

An article from Your Criminal Justice Network titled "Police Misconduct Cost Taxpayers over $3.2 Billion in Settlements" reports that, during the decade from 2010 to 2020, approximately 7,600 officers were alleged to have been involved in misconduct.

The Impact of Gun Violence on U.S. Citizens

In the Wikipedia article "Gun Violence in the United States," it is reported that "in 2016, a U.S. male aged 15–23 was 70 times more likely to be killed with a gun than a French or British male of the same age."

"In 2000, the costs of gun violence in the United States were estimated to be on the order of $100 billion per year."

"In 2022, up to 100 daily fatalities and hundreds of daily injuries were attributed to gun violence in the United States."

"The nation's largest and most comprehensive study into American firearms ownership found that privately owned firearms are used in roughly 1.7 million defensive usage cases (self-defense inside and outside the home) per year (2019–2021), and the CDC reported 20,958 homicides in 2021."

"Studies show that 'stand your ground' laws increase homicides. No rigorous study has yet determined that such laws deter violent crime."

"Between 1968 and 2011, approximately 1.4 million people died from firearms in the United States."

Should Americans continue living with these tragedies and costs, or should these outcomes no longer be accepted?

CHAPTER TWENTY-ONE

Within 24 hours after Mark sent his segment as an attachment, there was a resumption of the Zoom room dialogue.

Rx: Congratulations, Commander Jackson.ET: Wow! That's not like you, Doctor Graf, to congratulate someone.

PM: Hi folks. Yeah, Clyde, what have you been drinking?

SW: Thanks for your interesting segment, Mark. That history of policing sure taught me new things.

Rx: ET and PM, if you knew what I was comparing PM's segment to, you wouldn't come off as such wise guys. I'm pleased that Mark's segment is as short as it is—not long like KO's.

YY: Good afternoon, everyone. It's good to see you again. I hope you've all been healthy and enjoying yourselves.

KO: Hi, everyone. Mark, you have covered lots of ground with your segment. It contributes significantly to our work to persuade others to help make our country much safer.

ET: Yes, I agree with you, Roberto. I also gained a bit more appreciation for law enforcement, considering all the various entities police have had to deal with over the years: criminal gangs, murderers, protesters, mass shooters, etc.

SW: I can't imagine what it must have been like to be a night watchman in cold, rainy weather, without flashlights, mobile phones, or cars.

YY: It is good that you've been a police officer and can really appreciate all the various circumstances officers have experienced.

Rx: I think it's terrible what officers had to deal with those terrible protesters taking over the streets, blocking traffic, and not following orders from the police. Also, just like now, police had to deal with those dirty immigrants coming into the country in droves centuries ago.

KO: Clyde, that's called "free speech." We have the right, in the First Amendment, to assemble and speak freely. You must know that many of the immigrants who came to our country in the nineteenth century were Germans like yourself.

PM: Yes, we have lots of people who are violent, using the most modern types of firearms to commit crimes. So, with more training, better pay, mobile phones and two-way radios, better firearms, and bulletproof vests, being a police officer is still a very dangerous job—but safer.

SW: That Volker guy who introduced much more civility and better training for police conduct—we should be appreciative of people like him.

ET: Now, if we can do something much greater for civilization in mental health, education, parenting, and opportunities to become better citizens, that's our challenge now.

YY: Yes, Emily, I agree; however, there are other nations that are being challenged with many mental health issues, yet they don't suffer the homicide rates we do because they are dealing with guns differently than we do.

KO: Good point, Yoshi. I'm sure you'll provide us with much more relevant content on what you're addressing in your segment. That brings to mind: who is following Mark in presenting a segment?

SW: Mark, are you basically suggesting that even with all the advances in weaponry, communications, codes, training, means of travel, forensics, and everything else law enforcement now has to deal with criminals who have firearms, we are still really unable to prevent, control, and reduce the unlawful use of firearms in our country?

PM: Yes, Shahzad, that's a good summation of my segment. It's the availability of firearms and the misunderstood right to keep and bear arms that is the real problem.

ET: If we ever wish to complete this project and have it make some impact on our country, we need to think about moving on. Yoshi's and Shahzad's segments don't fit into the scheme of arguments at this point, so that just leaves you, Clyde, and me to be next to complete our segments and present them. I know you've presented yourself as being reluctant to present yours yet. Am I still perceiving your intentions correctly? If I am, that leaves me to be the next presenter.

KO: Thanks, Emily, for diligently offering to be next.

Rx: You got that right, ET. I'm not set yet to do the quintessential, definitive diagnosis regarding drug use. We definitely need to cut down on that estimated $10 billion in costs due to gun usage.

YY: Good idea, Emily. I'm inclined to support your reasoning. Shahzad and I should be the last to wrap up our project with our segments.

ET: Okay, if there are no objections, hopefully I'll send all of you gentlemen my segment soon. I'm trying to cover a lot of ground in it, which Clyde may object to, but we must try to convince as many citizens of our country as possible of our final proposal.

PM: With that said, unless anyone has a further comment, we can end this Zoom session so Emily and Clyde can have their dinners.

YY: Sayonara, everyone.

SW: Take care. Have a good journey in life.

KO: Gracias. Adiós, amigos. Thanks once more, Mark, for your insightful segment. It's a substantial contribution to our project!

EMILY THURMOND'S SEGMENT

Sleeping was a bit more challenging for me, and I woke up during the night many times thinking about creating this segment and the magnitude of importance surrounding it. It has been many years since I routinely sat down in my therapy office to counsel clients regarding their mental health and relationship concerns. Now I want to help counsel folks to do something to bring about a more civilized country and help in an evolution to eliminate the violent gun culture in the U.S. Here is my segment in this very significant project that I and the other senior citizens in the Zoom chat room have undertaken.

We as human beings have been conceived and developed along very complex and challenging paths and journeys to become what and who we are today. Human beings have been on this planet for a long time, in various parts of the world, with many scary fears to overcome, such as other creatures, the climate, the need for essentials such as food and water, and perhaps the greatest challenge of all: getting along and working with each other.

After many ancestral links, our grandparents, then parents, arrived as individuals and had to develop to a stage at which they were, if heterosexual, sexually attracted to the opposite sex. Each of the mates brought with her or him lots of baggage from their biological parents and ancestors, such as their ethnicity, skin pigmentation, body size, eye color, and DNA. And of course, their intellect and personality, as well as other variables such as incest and rape, which create other kinds of psychological baggage for them—and for us.

Their physical environment was also very important to their safety, comfort, ability to be educated, and general accommodation. Did the parents live in the desert of an African country? Were the parents living in a country at war with another country? Did the parents have a loving relationship with each other, their family, and friends? All these elements contributed to what the parents had to deal with, along with having a child come into their relationship and lives.

So, to put us on a healthy, successful path, with each parent bringing to the conception sperm cells and an egg to produce us, a whole lot of factors were in place. Was the sex that brought about the conception consensual? Were there loving feelings in both partners' hearts? Were they both at a stage of their own development to be capable, physically, mentally, and emotionally, of being beneficial and ready to take on the task of being parents? Would they be able, financially, to provide food, shelter, and a home for their offspring and be prepared to take on the challenges to her body during a pregnancy? Will the boyfriend or husband be restrained in his sexual impulses during the pregnancy? And, of course, will the mother's body stay in shape so as not to injure the embryo and then the fetus in any way by being a drug addict, alcoholic, under lots of stress, or by not having a healthy diet? Can she deal with the environmental challenges for nine months?

Now let's look at some issues the mother faces. According to an American Public Health Association paper, <u>"Birth Defects and Disabilities: A Public Health Issue for the 21st Century,"</u>

the report states, "The 20th century witnessed great advances in the diagnosis, treatment, and prevention of defects and developmental disabilities and in the quality of life and life expectancy of people living with disabilities." Some of the disabilities and defects include mental retardation, metabolic disorders, and, with surgical procedures, spina bifida and Down syndrome.

"Developmental disabilities result in social, emotional, behavioral, cognitive, and motor impairments… About 17 percent of children in the United States have a developmental disability, with about 2 percent having disabilities severe enough to require lifelong care…."

"Messages about proper nutrition, avoiding alcohol, tobacco, and some medications; ensuring adequate exercise; and properly managing chronic medical conditions should be included in a strategy for healthy pregnancies."

Now let's look at another component in conception with the article DNA *Is Not* Destiny, written by Steven J. Heine in 2017. "In the second week of April 2003, our world changed forever. We sequenced the first complete human genome. We each have a unique string of nucleotides in our cells that contributes to who we are. We are able to unravel this string and read it."

"Our genomes contain deep secrets about us: where our ancestors are from, which issues and diseases we'll likely avoid, and which ones might kill us, and what kinds of physical and psychological attributes we're predisposed to have."

"Aristotle famously proposed that each entity possesses an essence. Essences form the basis of identity for any entity, and they are the ultimate causes for why those entities function as they do."

"The most famous study to expose the relationship of the MAOA gene with violence… where researchers found that variations of child abuse led to a greater likelihood of violence."

Another contributing element to the mental health of our offspring is described in *Parental Maternal Stress and Offspring Aggressive Behavior: Intergenerational and Transgenerational Inheritance*, a paper from Frontiers in Behavioral Neuroscience.

"Prenatal maternal stress can arise from malnutrition, major life events, bereavement, depression, or anxiety. Prenatal stress may include poor dieting, illness, or could be ongoing events of life, like violent neighborhoods, ongoing wars, or sudden changes in a woman's daily routine."

"Brain imaging studies have shown that prenatal maternal stress is associated with significant thinning of the cortex and disruption of fundamental structural connections between the frontal cortex, the hippocampus, and the amygdala."

"The fetal HPA (hypothalamic-pituitary-adrenal) axis is fully developed and functional by the twenty-seventh week of pregnancy."

Stress on the HPA axis can lead to programming and expression of aggressive-like behavior in adult offspring.

Should the offspring and mother get through the pregnancy without a miscarriage or other severe injury, it's time for the delivery.

Whoopie!

Wait a moment. There are several complications that can arise in the delivery process. Labor can take longer than expected; perineal tears in the woman's body can occur; abnormal heart rates of the infant may develop; water may break too soon; and excessive bleeding, among other issues, must be dealt with quickly.

If a smooth childbirth delivery, vaginal, C-section, or other options, is performed, or if the complications can be dealt with successfully, parenting begins, no matter what the infant's condition is, whether the baby appears healthy or has an obvious physical debilitation. The parents' lives can be changed completely for the rest of their lives, hopefully in a very wonderful way.

Parenting:

However, as we know, most of us got our parenting training from our parents, which may have been very bad training. Here are some thoughts on parenting from experts and researchers.

Some online comments from first time parents:

1. Craig: "Being a dad is more challenging than I expected, but more rewarding than I ever expected."
2. "We found that a lot of people were a little too unsure to give their opinions, which were very strong," says Cameron. "Your instincts are usually correct."
3. "…parents remember to focus on each other rather than just focusing on the baby."
4. Consistency: "It really helps babies if they know what to expect—what's coming," says Laura.
5. Welcome the change in priorities.

Let's look at sleep, since infants sleep 14 to 17 hours per day.

In the review of Parenting Without Borders by Christina Gross-Loh, the following excerpts are from the book *The American Way*: "Our cultural belief about infant sleep is that it should be solitary, scheduled, independent, and fuss-free."

"The Swedish way of sleeping… co-sleeping is regarded positively. It is considered ordinary, so much so that it is not thought about consciously at all. They believe that if a child desires to sleep with a parent, if he wants to, it's good for him."

"The very best sleep happens when there is what researchers call 'goodness of fit,' the right match between a child's personality and parental expectations."

Now let's look at another significant element of parenting that is described in the next work:

Brain–Body Parenting: How to Stop Managing Behavior and Start Raising Joyful, Resilient Kids, the book by Mona Delahooke, PhD.

"19. 'The Platform.' In particular, behaviors provide clues about the state of a child's autonomic nervous system, the unique two-way system of communication between body and brain. The brain-body connection, our nervous system, serves as a neural platform that influences behavior."

"20. Parents have platforms too. … We know more about how stress manifests in the human body. When we consider the body and brain in a more integrated way, our children's and our own health and well-being benefit."

"42. 'If a child's safety system detects threat, we are likely to see behavior resulting from that reading. The child might refuse or resist doing something or have difficulty adapting to a situation.'"

"63. 'Green pathways: This pathway gives rise to a child's learning and growing, and to their own best parenting, and—when we reach a certain developmental ability, to control our emotions and behaviors.'"

"72. 'The blue pathway: disconnecting and withdrawing…. While the red pathway is associated with movement, the blue pathway is the opposite. Overwhelmed, a person conserves energy by withdrawing from connection and contact with the world.'"

"213. Tantrums: putting toddlers in context, calmly support children through frustration, disappointment, and even failure, so that we normalize these difficult but healthy life experiences."

"259. Benefits of play… We call play neural, or brain, exercise because it's a chance for children to process different sensations, feelings, and ideas under conditions of safety."

"273. Pathways to self-regulation… Once a child understands how to observe their body's reactions to the world, they can do something profound: practice solving problems both with you and on their own. When a child is able to recognize when their platform is getting vulnerable, a new level of self-sufficiency arises."

Okay, here are more suggestions on how to raise your kids well in order to prevent your child from developing aggressive behavior:

5 Ways Parents Can Raise Mentally Strong Kids, written by Amy Morin, a psychotherapist:

1. Make it a family priority to take care of your mind. Talk about the importance of caring for your minds. Make it a priority to build mental muscle, too. Perform mental-strength exercises as a family. You might need help from a professional.

2. Aside from 'anger' or 'excited,' most parents rarely mention feelings; consequently, kids aren't learning to identify their feelings or gaining the coping skills they need to deal with those feelings.

3. Teach your child how to think realistically. When your child expresses self-doubt or negative thoughts, teach him how to think differently. Show him how to recognize unhealthful thoughts and reframe them in a more realistic way...

4   Role-model to teach kids to take positive actions.... Kids need to know they can behave contrary to their feelings. In fact, their behavior can change their feelings.... Be a good role model and show your child that you behave contrary to your feelings sometimes. Say things like, 'I'm feeling kind of tired right now, but I know it's a good choice to go make dinner for us rather than just sit here and watch TV.'

5. Actively engage in problem-solving. It can be tempting to swoop in and solve kids' problems for them, but they need opportunities to practice problem-solving skills.... Natural consequences can be some of life's greatest teachers.... Solve problems together... brainstorming at least five solutions as a team...."

-

One other important factor that can be a beneficial aspect of successful parenting is discussed in an article from petrelationship. com, entitled "The Impact of Pets on Children's Development."

"Pets have been an integral part of human life for centuries, providing companionship, love, and joy to their owners. In households with children, pets play a significant role in shaping the development of young kids."

Emotional development: "Pets offer unconditional love and acceptance, creating a safe space where children can express their emotions freely.… This emotional bond fosters empathy, companionship, and a sense of responsibility, as children learn to care for and nurture their furry friends. Pets also play a critical role in helping children cope with stress and anxiety."

Social development: "Pets act as catalysts, encouraging children to engage in social interactions and develop important social skills.… Pets can also be a bridge between introverted children and their peers. For instance, a child who might find it challenging to initiate a conversation with other children may find it easier to approach them while walking a dog or playing with a pet."

Cognitive development: "By stimulating their curiosity and fostering a love for learning.… Additionally, studies have found that children who grow up with pets tend to have better verbal skills and a broader vocabulary. Conversations with pets provide a nonjudgmental space where children can practice speaking and storytelling without fear of criticism.…"

Physical development: "Dogs, in particular, require regular walking, exercise, or play, which can motivate children to engage in more physical activity.… Moreover, children who grow up with pets are more likely to develop better immune systems and have a reduced risk of allergies and asthma."

Now let us look at behavior issues and how best to deal with them as parents.

This information comes from the Child Mind Institute and is titled "Angry Kids: Dealing with Explosive Behavior," written by Vasco Lopes, PsyD.

"When a child, even a small child, melts down and becomes aggressive, they can pose a serious risk to themselves and others, including parents and siblings."

"It is helpful to first understand that behavior is communication. A child who is so overwhelmed that they are lashing out is a distressed child."

"…how you react when a child lashes out has an effect on whether they will continue to respond to distress in the same way or learn better ways to handle feelings so they don't become overwhelming. Some pointers: stay calm, help them with problem-solving, use time-outs and reward systems, and avoid triggers."

"…behavior therapies include parent–child interaction therapy, parent management therapy, and collaborative and proactive solutions."

When all of the above isn't enough:

Medication; learning how to use safe holds on your child; residential treatment facilities; and day treatment programs, a child with extreme behavior problems can attend a school that has trained staff to handle crisis situations safely.

Some possible reasons for aggressive behavior include ADHD, anxiety, undiagnosed learning disabilities, sensory processing issues, and autism.

Going beyond to three impactful causes of problematic development and bad behavior, excluding alcoholism and drug addiction in the household, are the following:

1. Domestic violence in the home

2. Living in a neighborhood with violence

3. Social media

The following is taken from the Children's Domestic Violence Association article "How Does Domestic Violence Impact Children?"

"In homes with domestic violence, children are negatively impacted at all stages of their development in key areas of life: physically, mentally, behaviorally, and emotionally."

"Symptoms related to children growing up with domestic violence:

Newborns to age 5: sleep or eating disorders; intense separation anxiety; increased aggression and/or impulsive behavior.

Ages 6–11: aggression and difficulty with peer relationships; withdrawal and/or emotional numbing; school avoidance and truancy.

Ages 12–18: antisocial behavior; impulsive and/or reckless behavior; substance abuse; involvement in violent and abusive dating relationships."

"Studies have concluded that experiencing domestic violence is sufficient trauma to contribute to post-traumatic stress disorder (PTSD) in children."

"Moms facing domestic violence before and during pregnancy are also up to six times more likely to develop postpartum depression, as well as triggering cognitive and behavioral problems in their children."

"Outcomes… Without help from a caring adult or improvement in the home, children are more likely to experience negative outcomes. For example: six times more likely to commit suicide, 50 percent more likely to abuse alcohol or drugs, and 74 percent more likely to commit a violent crime."

"As many as 10 million children and adolescents witness domestic violence between their parents or caregivers yearly."

One more source of information comes from a study entitled *How Domestic Violence Affects Children?*, presented by the National Child Traumatic Stress Network:

"People living with handgun owners died by homicide at twice the rate of their neighbors in gun-free homes."

"People living with handgun owners were seven times more likely to be shot by their spouse or intimate partner…"

"…the vast majority of victims in these intimate partner shootings—84 percent in all—were female."

"The results of the research study clash with a classic narrative promulgated by gun-rights groups: firearm owners use their weapons to turn away or overpower threatening intruders, thereby protecting home and health. We did not detect even a hint of such protective benefits."

A circumstance that can certainly impact a child's development **in** a very negative way, yet is not always possible for parents to control, is living in poverty and in neighborhoods where there is extensive drug use, vandalism, and gang violence.

Neighborhood: The following is from an article, *Living with Neighborhood Violence May Shape Teens' Brains*, written by Darby and *The Conversation*:

"More than half of children and adolescents living in cities have experienced some form of community violence, acts of disturbance or crime, such as drug use, beatings, shootings, and stabbings in their neighborhoods or schools."

"Over time, living with the stress of community violence may lead children to become less engaged in school, withdraw from friends, or show symptoms of post-traumatic stress, such as irritability and intrusive thoughts. In short, living in an unsafe community can have a corrosive effect on child development."

"In other words, our research participants told us that around age 13 their neighborhoods were higher in crime and violence; the size of these critical brain structures—the hippocampus and amygdala—looked smaller about four years later, compared to teens who reported less community violence."

Now let us look at why kids join neighborhood gangs and what they get out of joining, as described in the article Why Do Youth Join Gangs? from the Office of Juvenile Justice and Delinquency Prevention.

"Social, economic, and cultural forces push many adolescents in the direction of gangs. Protection from other gangs and perceived well-being are key factors…. Feeling marginalized, adolescents join gangs for social relationships that give them a sense of identity…. Some are intensely recruited or coerced into gangs."

So some teens living in neighborhoods with gangs may feel pressured or have a sense of need to belong and join a gang. Now let us take this a step further and look at what could be happening in the future of this gang member.

From the Johns Hopkins Annual Firearms Data, an article entitled Gun Violence in the U.S., 2022: Examining the Burden Among Children and Teens states:

"Trend over time… The overall gun death rates among youths doubled between 2013 and 2022. This rise is predominantly attributable to an increase in gun homicides across age subgroups, though suicides are also increasing among teens (ages 10–17) and among young adults (ages 18–19)."

"Racial disparities **in** gun deaths over time: In 2022, Black youths had a gun death rate six times higher than their white counterparts. Hispanic/Latino gun death rates increased nearly twice as much as those of their white counterparts from 2013 to 2022."

Social media:

Most parents and teachers know teens access social media platforms far too much, but do they know how threatening that behavior can be and the impact it can have on teens' development and behavior?

Here is some information from an article from the Cleveland Clinic entitled How Social Media Can Negatively Affect Your Child (January 2024):

"Most social media apps require users to be at least 13 years old. But according to the U.S. Surgeon General, nearly 40 percent of children ages 8 to 12 and 95 percent of children ages 13 to 17 use social media apps."

"The U.S. Surgeon General released an advisory on how social media affects children's and teenagers' mental health. The scariest statistic? Teens who spend more than three hours a day on social media double their risk of depression and anxiety."

Suggestions for parents:

"Determine if your child is ready."

"Talk with your kids."

"Limit screen time."

Some serious issues with kids being on social media include:

"Body image concerns."

"Cyberbullying."

"Online predators."

"Changes in daily behavior:"

1. Increased irritability.
2. Increased anxiety.
3. Increased depression.
4. Increased sleep issues.
5. Lack of self-esteem.

"Lack of focus and concentration."

Another source of information relating to the harm social media does to teens is covered in the book The Anxious Generation, written by Jonathan Haidt.

"The first explanation for this generation is about the decline in the play-based childhood, which began in the 1980s and accelerated in the 1990s…. Many parents in Anglo countries began to reduce children's access to unsupervised outdoor free play. The second story is about the rise of the phone-based childhood beginning in the late 2000s and accelerating in the early 2010s…. Adolescents traded in their flip phones for smartphones, which were loaded with social media platforms supported by the new high-speed internet and unlimited data plans."

"The sudden increase in anxiety and depression wasn't merely a heightened willingness to talk about mental illness. The rise was showing up in behavior as well, including in self-harm and suicide."

Some of the author's suggestions to help prevent the negative effects of smartphone abuse are:

- "Give children far more time playing with other children."
- "Look for more ways to embed children in stable, real-world communities."
- "Don't give a smartphone as the first phone."
- "Don't give a smartphone until high school."

Red Flag Laws:

Should social media negatively affect your child or teen, should you check out red flag laws? Here are some facts about the usage of and help provided by such laws.

Here are some findings from the article Recognizing Red Flags in Behavior: A *Guide* for *Parents* and *Caregivers*, by Sherri Gordon Calca:

"When it comes to recognizing whether or not your teen's mental health is suffering, most experts we talked with say that if your gut is telling you something is wrong, then likely something is wrong. And the sooner you address the issue, the better off your teen will be."

"For instance, changes in behavior might include isolating oneself from peers, poor academic performance, or overindulging in social media. Other red flags might include changes in appearance, which can range from a sudden shift in style or dress to failure to maintain hygiene."

"It's not uncommon to see teens struggle with their mental health. Teenagers can have an impairing mental health disorder."

"Any comments about self-harm, hopelessness about the future, or remarks about wanting to die should be taken seriously and addressed immediately by a mental health professional."

"Parents should always reach out to medical professionals or use the 988 hotline if the situation reaches a point at which they are concerned about the safety or life of their child."

Unfortunately, some parents do not take the advice aforementioned, or they ignore it, or even worse, stimulate bad behavior in certain ways. Let's look at an extreme case of this. In the article entitled Are Parents to Blame for the Crimes of Their Kids?, presented by Michelle Charles, JD, PsyD, LCSW:

"The answer is… a resounding yes. Parents can be legally liable for the criminal actions of their children."

"On Nov. 30, 2021, Jennifer and James Crumbley's son, Ethan, opened fire at Oxford High School in Michigan, killing four students and wounding seven."

Red Flags Ignored by Ethan's Parents

1. Jennifer ignored a text Ethan sent her regarding being worried about an intruder in their home.
2. He appeared to "hallucinate," writing, "The house is haunted."
3. Ethan told a friend that he thought about calling 911, but he believed his parents would be upset.
4. In his journal, he wrote, "Fighting my dark side… my parents won't listen to me about help or a therapist."

Not only did Ethan's parents ignore all the red flags regarding his behavior, they also provided him with a gun.

"Studies reveal that youth violence is typically associated with family dynamics, neurological factors, academic achievement, personality traits, exposure to media violence, alcohol and drug abuse, social rejection, mental health issues, and access to guns."

Some critics believe holding parents accountable for crimes committed by their children is not the answer to preventing crime. They argue we should focus on "societal problems that demand greater attention."

The parents were found guilty of involuntary manslaughter and sentenced to several years of incarceration.

With all the aforementioned information, how should we proceed from here? I believe education, therapy, love, and community may help us—and the country—better understand what sex, conception, and parenting are all about.

Teenagers, 13 and older, should be educated on all the consequences of sexual behavior. Heterosexual, homosexual, and transgender youth should be taught what is relevant to them.

Kids should know about the dynamics involved in sexual arousal, hormones, and emotional factors between two individuals.

There is much information available online and in classes in high schools and middle schools. The following is information parents and teens can use to further educate teenagers. Here's an example:

<u>Teens and Sex: What Every Teen Should Know,</u> Univision, Nov. 2015

"Nowadays, children are exposed to the idea of sex at a very young age, sometimes when they are *even* 8 or 11 years old."

"The media and society are usually the first contributors when it comes to children learning about sex."

"The only thing that we can do as parents is to teach our teens the facts they need to know to keep themselves safe and healthy. Here are some of the basics that every teenager should know…"

Sex is not a way to show how mature or grown up you are; an abusive act; something you should do by a certain age to be cool; a way to prove your love to someone or to make somebody love you; a way to show you are committed to someone; an act of manipulation; a smart way to show your independence to your parents or get back at them; or an act of revenge against another person. It is **not** always a pleasurable act, as it can be painful, messy, and even noisy. Sex should occur between two consenting individuals, yet it is extremely risky: you can catch an STD, get pregnant, or feel extremely disappointed and let down when it is over. You may feel shame and guilt, or even be heartbroken. It is best when shared between two people who love and care for each other.

In sex-ed classes, boys need to learn about condoms and how to use them, and parents need to make sure their daughters can obtain birth control if they intend to participate in sexual activities.

However, should a teen daughter become pregnant due to unprotected sexual relations, what should parents and she know and do? This is the subject of the following article:

What Should I *Teach My High School–Aged Teen About Pregnancy* and *Reproduction?*, presented by Planned Parenthood.

"Teens whose parents talk with them about sex, birth control, preventing STDs, and pregnancy are more likely to wait to have sex, use condoms when they do have sex, and avoid unintended pregnancy."

"Tell them that no matter what happens, you love them and they can come to you in any situation."

"The average age of first sex is 17. But it's never too early to make sure your teen knows what's up when it comes to birth control and condoms. Like all pregnant people, pregnant teens have three options: abortion, adoption, and parenting."

"Parents of teens whose partner has become pregnant can support their teens as they figure out their new responsibilities. Teens whose partner becomes pregnant don't get to decide if their partner has an abortion or gives birth. Teen fathers are expected to provide child support, like fathers over age 18, and may need help handling new financial responsibilities."

"You may be worried about your own ability to help with money or childcare. Setting expectations and boundaries from the start can help you and your teen avoid conflict in the future. But while you think about the kind of help you can offer, try not to let any anger you *may* have about the situation prevent you from seeing how important your help is."

Now let us look at what may happen after conception and during the prenatal period, the entire time of a pregnancy. It is during this time that major complications can inflict serious, lifelong physical and/or emotional ailments, including brain development in ways that may create a possibility of aggressive behavior extending to gun violence.

In <u>Pregnancy Statistics</u>, written by Becca Stanek: "The majority of pregnancies go smoothly. However, as those who have experienced pregnancy complications know, that's not always the case. In around 8 percent of pregnancies, complications occur that could result in harm to the mother or baby if they are not treated."

"Ectopic pregnancy, which is when the fetus develops outside the uterus, occurs in about 1 in 50 pregnancies. Miscarriages happen in around 15 percent of pregnancies, and they are usually because of chromosomal abnormalities." Other pregnancy complications include hypertension, depression and anxiety, placental abruption, and more.

"Maternal mortality in the U.S. is increasing, with an estimated 17.4 maternal deaths for every 100,000 live births, due to complications related to pregnancy or childbirth…. The rate of maternal mortality in the U.S. is more than twice that of other high-income countries."

"The rate of maternal mortality for non-Hispanic Black women in the U.S. is almost three times that of white women, at 55.3 deaths per 100,000 live births. Rates of maternal mortality increase markedly by age, with the rate for women over 40 almost eight times higher than the rate for women under the age of 25."

Now let us read an article that answers questions such as "How does a baby's brain develop during pregnancy?" and "Why is brain development important during pregnancy?" under the title *Becoming* a Family.

"Your baby's brain is one of the first organs to form, beginning early in pregnancy and developing rapidly. By four weeks post-conception, the foundation for the brain and spinal cord are already established…. Women often report experiencing symptoms associated with 'pregnancy brain' early in the first trimester, coinciding with hormone fluctuations commonly described as 'baby brain.'"

"Fetal cranial growth observed between 20 and 25 weeks is a significant period for brain development. The brain, part of the central nervous system, undergoes significant development, and the prefrontal cortex experiences significant synaptic growth…."

The size and all the components of the brain continue to develop until birth. It's amazing what happens in the womb over nine months of pregnancy. What is also amazing is all the various factors that begin developing in terms of the behavior of each human being. The point of this segment is the element of aggression, which can lead to violence. The following article deals with that element of behavior.

From Cutting-Edge Psychology Insights, the article "Aggressive Behavior in Psychology: Causes and Underlying Factors" states:

"From deep within the human psyche, a tempestuous force lies dormant, waiting for the right triggers to unleash its fury upon the world: aggressive behavior. This primal instinct, deeply rooted in our evolutionary past, can manifest in myriad ways, from subtle microaggressions to full-blown violent outbursts. But what exactly is aggressive behavior, and why does it continue to plague our modern society?"

"Let's dive into the murky waters of our biochemical makeup. Our genes, which hold the tiny building blocks of life, play a significant role in shaping our propensity for aggression…. Hormones also have a say in the matter."

"Testosterone has long been associated with aggressive behavior."

"Now, let's talk about the command center in all our brains…. Neuroscientists have been poking and prodding at our brain matter, trying to unravel the mysteries of aggressive behavior. They've found that certain areas of the brain, like the amygdala and the prefrontal cortex (our impulse-control center), play a crucial role in regulating aggression."

"Moving from biology to psychology, a whole new set of factors contributes to aggressive behavior. One of the most well-known theories is the frustration–aggression hypothesis. Our thoughts play a huge role, too. Cognitive distortions can fuel aggressive behavior…. Emotional regulation is another key player, and personality disorders can significantly increase the likelihood of aggressive behavior."

"As we have seen, aggressive behavior is a complex phenomenon with roots in biology, psychology, and the social environment. Understanding this multifaceted nature of aggression is crucial for developing effective prevention and intervention strategies."

In my closing of this segment, I feel it incumbent upon me to summarize all of this so that the research, experiences, and data can effectively impact our mission to significantly reduce the suffering, deaths, and culture of violent gun use in our country. This can be achieved by reducing aggressive behavior through relevant education for teens, prenatal care and knowledge, healthy parenting, effective schools, and a society that develops healthy kids, promotes peace, provides better poverty relief in neighborhoods, encourages healthy diets, sets proper limits on social media, and enforces necessary limitations on gun ownership.

We shouldn't needlessly allow many thousands of deaths due to gun violence to occur in our blessed country each year!

CHAPTER TWENTY-TWO

It was two days following Emily's transmission of her segment to her Zoom room participants when she received an email from Roberto suggesting they all come together again at their usual time to meet later that day. She had many thoughts in her mind about missing something she should have included, wondering how her fellow Zoom room project friends would react to her segment, and whether they thought it would substantially contribute to their goal of convincing Americans to support major changes in America's gun culture. As she clicked the link to enter the room, she soon found Roberto and Yoshi already there.

KO: Welcome, Emily! It's a pleasure to see you again.

VY: Yes, Emily, congratulations on creating a powerful and very informative segment.

ET: Many thanks to you both. I'm glad to see you again after a few weeks. What have you two been doing?

YY: Thanks for asking. I've been spending some time considering various approaches to my segment.

PM: Hi, everybody! I'm glad to resume contact with all of you, and I'm especially—

KO: Emily, I got a chance to visit an uncle in Peru, who lives in a beautiful city named Arequipa, also called the "White City."

Rx: Okay, you laggards, let's get on with reviewing and critiquing ET's work.

KO: You've done it again, Clyde. You enter the room without any acknowledgment of those present and without any courtesy.

PM: Emily, I like your approach with regard to dealing with how killers become killers—from childbirth, parenting, neighborhoods, domestic violence, and the rest of the things that contribute to terrible outcomes.

SW: Greetings, fellow pundits. It's good to be with you again in this room. Emily, I am very impressed by and interested in your narrow focus when it comes to what brings about individuals who wind up killing others intentionally—not in self-survival or in wartime.

ET: Thank you, Shahzad, for your positive critique. It just makes sense to me, from my perspective in psychology, to look at the issue in terms of what develops in the human mind and emotions and how that development brings about an intention to harm others. We have many avenues through which human sensitivity can provoke some kind of hurt, such as scamming, hacking, robbery, rape, etc. We need to study this development much more.

PM: One of the thoughts that came to my mind as I read your segment regarding the three situations that can cause this negative aggression in kids, especially boys, is the fact that many kids are being raised by single mothers who often lose control of their parenting by the time a child is a teen. Those kids, usually boys, no longer pay attention to their mother's requests or scolding; they hit the streets and become violators of the law. I witnessed this many times while on the force in Pasadena.

Rx: Are you suggesting ET go back and amend her segment to include your experiences?

PM: No, Clyde. I'm only recalling some situations involving kids who can get into trouble without strong fatherly parenting.

ET: Thanks for remembering your experiences, Mark. Some of what you say may be included in the problems associated with gang-related neighborhoods. It's really awful that some kids are raised in those neighborhoods, especially without fathers living with them.

KO: Your segment is well structured, pointing out so much of the development of kids. There are so many factors involved.

YY: Emily, your segment points out that it is not only the gun violence culture our country needs to resolve; it is also the aggressive nature and violent behavior of many young guys in our country. So, we have two connected challenges, don't we?

ET: Very good observations, Yoshi and Mark. Yes, to do something about the gun violence problem, we must also focus on the aggressive behavior that is brewing during the development of too many young men. Years ago, a book entitled Pedagogic Logic was published that offered a very revolutionary reformation of our educational system in this country. The reforms would significantly reduce juvenile delinquency, reduce the distraction of social media, and reduce the attraction of street gangs by allowing students to choose what they would learn, along with parents and counselors serve as interns on jobs, train while also being in classrooms, be paid for their time in both settings, and become first-class citizens.

SW: Wow! That would be revolutionary! Would the kids still learn their ABCs, math, and other academic parts of the current school curriculum?

Rx: Come on, stop talking about some lunatic idea that ET can add to the minutiae in the segment. You need to be giving her suggestions to diminish the length of her segment. How many readers are going to read all of her embellishments?

PM: Knock it off, Clyde! We're trying to have a sensible conversation, and you want us to hurry through it so you can get on with presenting your segment about drugs' influence on gun crime. Be patient.

YY: Emily, another observation I focused on was how much females have to deal with, as opposed to males not having anything like that to deal with. Females have to deal with menstruation for over thirty years of their lives. If they get pregnant, they have to deal with something growing inside their bodies for nine months, then go through childbirth, which can be very painful. Then the mother has to devote all of her attention for a while to nursing the baby and then being responsible for feeding, changing diapers, etc., for years. What does the father do? Hold the female's hand, pay some bills, and perhaps change a diaper or two or feed the baby. My perspective is that men, in general, must learn about what females have to deal with, truly appreciate it, and offer complete support and comfort.

Rx: What is this becoming? There's not a single word about our mission to do something about the gun culture in America!

SW: Thank you, Yoshi, for bringing this to our attention. It is of foremost importance!

KO: If our country can learn what other nations are doing differently from what we do in our culture, we will be taking a giant step toward changing our violent gun culture.

KO: I sincerely wish you, Yoshi, much fortitude and good research information to bring your discoveries to all of us and to the country.

Rx: KO, in your remarks, you seem to be diminishing the element of drugs as a major cause of the gun violence this country is suffering from. Is that capricious on your part, or is it just disdain?

ET: Okay, gentlemen, I very much appreciate your interest and comments regarding my segment. It's been great seeing all of you, and I'm very much looking forward to reading your segment on drugs' influence on gun violence, Clyde; your segment, Yoshi, on what the rest of the civilized world is doing to have less gun violence; and Shahzad's on what you come up with, as an engineer, as a final solution structure for the country to transition toward making our country safe, with much less access to guns, sustainable laws, and workable law enforcement. I'm going to make dinner now. Best wishes. Good evening.

PM: Okay, Clyde, it's your turn. Good luck in making us proud and successful in our mission.

KO: No disdain or capriciousness. I ditto Mark's remarks.

YY: I'm looking forward to learning a lot from your pharmacology, Clyde.

Rx: Don't expect a long-winded segment like those already presented.

CLYDE'S GRAF SEGMENT

It was a little past 5:00 a.m. when Clyde exited his king-sized bed and went directly to his medicine cabinet to swallow a couple of pills. He wanted to make this a special day in that he was going to send his segment to his Zoom room associates. He had completed his quintessential, superior, and succinct presentation on the affiliation between narcotics and homicides. He sent the document after having breakfast and then waited until 7:00 a.m. EST.Dr. Clyde Grafs segment

Pharmaceuticals can be life-saving or life-destroying, depending on what they are and how they are used. They can be used in medical facilities to relieve patients suffering severe pain, or they can be used on the street to relieve pain or provide feelings of euphoria. Most are legally sold and used, yet some are grown or mixed through very illegal and unsafe production, destroying lives, including being involved in provoking a person to commit homicide with a firearm.

Other terms used for pharmaceuticals are drugs, medications, and narcotics. They can all be misused if not taken as prescribed by a medical doctor or pharmacist.

The federal agency named the Food and Drug Administration, otherwise known as the FDA, is charged with evaluating drugs and allowing them to be placed on the U.S. market for use. The FDA determines whether a drug is safe and effective for its intended use. The administration has approved about 20,000 drugs over many years. However, many of the approved prescription drugs have been altered or taken off the market over time.

Drugs coming from other countries must be approved by the FDA before being sold and used in the United States. Most of these drugs come from countries such as Canada, the Netherlands, Colombia, and Bolivia.

Unfortunately, most of the international, illegally produced drugs entering the United States come from Mexican cartels, which grow plant-based drugs such as cocaine and heroin or acquire basic ingredients for synthetic, designer, or stimulant drugs such as fentanyl and methamphetamine from China. Of course, these drugs are not inspected by the FDA before being put on the black market. Drug *trafficking* is the term used for importing illegal drugs into the United States. The most popular and common illegal drugs are methamphetamines, powdered cocaine, fentanyl, heroin, and crack cocaine.

It is estimated that the illicit opioid market alone cost Americans $1.7 trillion in 2023. That is big business, and the profiteers are not going to back away or give up easily.

The five countries with the worst drug abuse problems, in order from worst to least, are Iran, Afghanistan, Russia, the United States, and Great Britain.

Americans buy and use more prescribed pharmaceuticals per capita than citizens of any other country. In 2023, Americans spent over $700 billion. The average per capita drug spending in the United States was $1,432 in 2021. Italians, who buy a large amount of prescription drugs, spent $820 per capita in 2023, making them second to the United States.

How do those illegal, illicit, non-prescribed drugs impact the user's brain to trigger gun violence?

Methamphetamines, cocaine, and other brain stimulants such as heroin can provoke hyperactivity, creating neurotoxicity that can lead to impulsivity affecting cognitive thinking, agitation, and aggression in the prefrontal cortex, which can bring on violent behavior.

This is just one scenario of how illegal drug use, especially by young people, particularly male teens and young men, over time can increase the risk of violent behavior such as homicide.

So, the pertinent questions are what our society and culture need to do to take on these challenges to reduce the availability, access, and lure of illegal drugs and alcohol in order to reduce the number of homicides, mass shootings, and harmful gun use.

The three objectives are:

1. Prevention, or forestalling the use of illegal, harmful drugs
2. Drug addiction, dealing with someone who has developed an addiction to illegal drugs
3. Treatment for withdrawal from drug addiction

A "War on Drugs" in the United States began in 1971. The prison population began to grow substantially in 1973, and thereafter the rate of illegal drug use went up for a while and stabilized in the 1990s. Many illicit drug abuse rehabilitation centers have been created. According to Google, most individuals who have been treated in the United States have been successful in getting off drugs and staying off.

1. Prevention and forestalling:

First, do not become a parent until you have completed the education you need to acquire a good-paying job, find a loving partner, and get married.

Then find a house, condo, or apartment that you can afford to buy or lease in a good, healthy neighborhood, not a gang-infected one, and check out the schools. If you have to wait a while to find or afford one, don't get pregnant.

Both parents need to be excellent role models for any children they give birth to. That means not having any addictions to alcohol or illegal drugs, not smoking of any kind, and not using vulgar language around the kids. Also, don't in any way abuse each other with harsh language or violence.

Have friends, including family members, who are raising children appropriately be part of your extended family. Introduce your kids to healthy activities such as sports, religion, and creative pursuits. They need to be part of peer groups that are not going to influence them to use illegal drugs in any way.

As for education and schools, look for good areas with good schools. Instill motivation in your kids, by example, to want to learn, be curious, and succeed. That radical book Pedagogic Logic offers ideas to help motivate kids to really want to learn and benefit from their learning.

Most importantly, our kids need to know and feel that you, as parents, truly love them so they can trust and believe that you are on their side when they need you.

2. Addiction: Parents need to be able to observe and recognize changes in their teen's behavior, mood, friendships, and schoolwork in order to realize there may be a problem with illegal drugs. Why not just sit down and ask your teens, in a caring and concerned manner, if he or she is having a problem you may be able to assist with? It is not about being judgmental, just being helpful. If you have noted that she or he is hanging out with new friends, you might ask why and who they are. If any grades at school are down, why not ask why and speak to the teachers? If any significant changes in attitude, interests, or activities have been noticed, ask why without being negative. Your child needs to believe and know that you are on his or her side. If you learn that there is a problem with drug abuse, you then need to learn about and offer the treatment needed to withdraw from such use before it becomes a greater, more serious problem that could lead to medical issues, problems at school, or trouble with the law.

3. Treatments: Whether your teen reveals to you that he or she is hooked on narcotics or not, if you suspect it, you should know about a medication that can be used in case there is an overdose. It is known as Narcan, or by its OTC name, naloxone, which can counteract the effects of opioid overdoses. Insofar as various treatments are available, you can check online for what is available with regard to the severity of the addiction. If need be, you can place your teens in a detox center or rehab facility for 30 to 90 days, depending on what is needed for success. It is not inexpensive, possibly up to $14,000. The success rate of some residential drug rehab centers is as high as 95 percent.

Once your child is no longer addicted to illegal drugs, what should you as parents, and he or she, do to stay free from drug abuse? Family therapy should be considered to help understand what motivated the child to become addicted in the first place. You can also think about more activities the family can do together, such as traveling, going to sports games and plays, looking into colleges or trade schools for the teen to enroll in, and checking out community organizations and support groups. The teen should also consider doing some part-time work with his or her parents, neighbors, or within the community. If you are inclined, think about spiritual organizations, service clubs, or sports the child can become involved in. The teen needs to become more responsible for the decisions made and actions taken.

Lastly, the teen needs to develop an attitude of respect for firearms that will prevent him or her from even considering owning a firearm to hurt someone else. This is the whole point of this segment. Keep firearms away from anyone who may be in a mental state to use a gun to hurt someone, including the parent or the teen himself or herself.

In one study, as many as 86 percent of those involved in homicides in the United States had a connection to drug use. This needs to be dealt with urgently!

CHAPTER TWENTY-THREE

YY: Doctor Graf, it's remarkable that you produced so much in such a short segment and in such a small amount of time.

SW: Yes, Yoshi, it took the others weeks to produce their segments, and look how quickly the doctor wrote his.

RX: Okay, you guys, show some appreciation for not having to wait as long as I had to wait for the other guys. I was trying to be succinct and solicitous, not showing off how many words I could include.

ET: Thank you, Clyde, for a very informative and convincing segment. It will definitely increase the value of our mission!

Rx: Thanks, ET, for those conciliatory remarks that offset some of the negativity I've received in the room.

KO: Good afternoon, everyone. It's nice seeing all of you again. I also thought there would be a longer time between our Zoom sessions; however, knowing Clyde as I do, I'm not at all surprised that he was able to produce his segment in a much shorter time than the rest of us. Congratulations, Clyde.

PM: I guess I've missed some of your remarks, everyone, but it's good seeing you again. Clyde, I learned some things about drug abuse and how much Americans rely on drugs in general. While serving as a police officer, I encountered many gang members who were strung out on illegal drugs.

ET: It is inconceivable that we have the drug problems we do in this country. So many people rely on opioids or painkillers to relieve their aches and pains rather than doing something about what causes those issues.

SW: I admire how you structured the three "big questions." The information is very important to be aware of and to implement.

YY: Emily and Clyde, why is it that Americans buy and use more drugs than citizens in other countries? That's an important observation and question.

Rx: I can tell you this, Yoshi: we create more drugs and put them on the market much sooner than most other countries. Doctors and those suffering from various conditions are awaiting relief.

YY: Obesity must be one of the problems we have here. When I travel to Japan, I don't see many people looking as overweight as I do here.

PM: I just checked the stats, Yoshi. Japan has an obesity rate of about 4 percent, and the U.S. has an obesity rate of 42 percent. That's why you can discern the difference between the two nations.

KO: I am amazed by the facts you presented regarding treatment, the level of withdrawal success, and the amount of time it requires.

Rx: Yes, KO, it's remarkable. Now it's getting to be time to have YY or SW commit to writing their segment next.

PM: Clyde, you didn't mention the percentage of homicides related to street gangs in the U.S. Those homicides are primarily due to illegal drug issues. They amount to an estimated 13 or 14 percent of all homicides.

SW: I actually would have guessed a higher percentage. What is it for something like domestic violence?

ET: I think we've already mentioned that the percentage can be as high as 20 percent of all murders in our country being due to guns in a household where there is domestic violence.

Rx: Whoa! You guys are going off track. I thought I mentioned the various problems involving drug addiction. My goal was to present solutions to the problems.

KO: You did, Doctor. Obviously, the doctor feels he is being critiqued and isn't welcoming it. He gave us a lot of good information for the readers of our proposal to absorb. Maybe Yoshi will give us some vital information for us to use as well.

PM: Okay, Roberto. However, I want to restate my concern about the need for teen boys to have their dads' involvement in their lives.

ET: Thumbs up on that, Mark. Now it's on to Yoshi. Good wishes, and we'll be eagerly awaiting your segment.

YY: Well, unless Clyde or anyone else has anything to say, I thank you all for your trust in me to produce something that will contribute to our success.

SW: Best wishes! Go for it, Yoshi!

Rx: Voluminous, YY, is not the key to success. Stick to succinctness.

YOSHI YAMAMOTO' SEGMENT

1. Pursuant to my outline, countries that have a constitutional right, a Second Amendment–type right, to own and bear arms are limited. According to a Google search, there are only three countries that currently offer this right: the United States, Mexico, and Guatemala. Other countries in the past have had such a constitutional right but have since abandoned it.

2. Gun ownership in other countries vs. the U.S.: India has about 71 million firearms; China, 50 million; Mexico, 20 million; Russia, 18 million; Germany, 5 million; Japan, 310,000; Brazil, 18 million; South Africa, 2 million; and the United States has about 393 million.

3. Homicide rates in countries with no right to own firearms: Except for very few nations, most countries do not recognize a right of firearm ownership. First, among countries that ban ownership, reliable data on actual ownership are not available, including Cambodia, North Korea, China, and several others. Homicide rates are as follows: Cambodia, 2.4 per 100,000 population; North Korea, data not reliable; China, 0.50 per 100,000 population.

4. Countries that have a partial ban or limited rights to own a firearm: Japan, Norway, and the United Kingdom. Homicide rates are as follows: Japan, 0.23 per 100,000 population; Norway, 0.72; and the United Kingdom, 1.00. The U.S. homicide rate is 5.7 per 100,000 population (with no bans or limited rights).

5. Laws denying citizens the right to own a firearm in other countries: In Cambodia, the law titled The Management of Weapons, Explosives and Ammunition and the Equipping of Firearms denies citizens the possession and carrying of all types of weapons. Japan has very rigid gun ownership laws. Handguns are prohibited, and only shotguns and rifles for hunting are permitted to be owned.

6. What are the crime rates involving guns in countries that allow guns to be owned easily versus those that don't allow gun ownership or impose significant restrictions: U.S.:

	Homicides	Robberies
U.S	72%	40%
Mexico	71	68
Cambodia	13	67 (2003)
Japan	0	10 or less

7. Which developed countries like the United States have a similar gun violences culture? Let us check Germany, Scotland, France, South

Korea and Switzerland: homicides per 100,000 population. Germany (0.833), Scotland (10.4 per million), France (0.24–0.4), South Korea (0.00005), Switzerland (0.11), and the United States (5.6).

Maybe this is a good place to inquire why so many Americans feel the need to possess a firearm. The answer, according to many studies, is mostly for self-protection and self-defense.

Is this the case in other developed countries? Germans own guns for hunting, sport shooting, and collection. In France, firearms are owned for hunting, sport shooting, and self-protection.

8. What is the incarceration situation and what rehabilitation programs exist? This is applicable only to those convicted and sentenced for gun violence.

The U.S. has roughly 25 percent of the world's federal and state prisoners combined—about 1,230,000—with approximately 375,500 convicted of using or possessing a firearm during a crime.

Contrast those figures with Germany, India, Japan, and Spain:

Germany: total incarcerated, 58,000; fewer than 2 percent, or less than 1,200, used a firearm to commit their crimes.

India: total prisoners, 573,000; data unavailable.

Japan: 40,500; with about 10 homicides per year, gun-related crimes and the number of prisoners are very low.

Spain: 56,500; data not found, but low.

Juvenile detentions: U.S., 48,000; Germany, 3,000; India, about 35,000; Japan, 5,500; Spain, 14,000.

<u>Rehabilitation policies and recidivism</u>

U.S.: Each state and the federal government has policies intended to reduce repeat convictions and returns to prison. Rehabilitation policies include job training, psychological therapy, education, and relationship training for family and community reintegration. The recidivism rate is 66 percent within three years.

Germany: Rehabilitation programs include resocialization, education, vocational training, and community reintegration support. The recidivism rate is 33 percent.

India: Rehabilitation programs include vocational training, social reintegration, counseling, and religious classes. The recidivism rate ranges from 4 to 8 percent over the past few years.

Japan: Rehabilitation programs include a tailored, individual approach; group therapy; and age-related, individualized programs.

Recidivism rate: 47 percent, mostly among the elderly.

Spain: Rehabilitation policies focus on education and resocialization.

Recidivism rate: The "open" regime rate is 18 percent, while the "closed" regime rate is 45 percent. Prisoners in the open regime are allowed to work outside prison facilities and, with good behavior, may even live at home.

9. How are the educational systems in low-homicide-rate nations different from that of the U.S.?

Let us look at Finland, Switzerland, Japan, and China.

Mathematics global ranking by country:
U.S., 26th; Finland, 20th; Switzerland, 8th; Japan, 5th; China, 15th (based on 15-year-old students).

Average spending per student per school year:
U.S., $18,000+ (2020–21); Finland, $11,000+; Switzerland, $20,000 (2023); Japan, $10,000 (primary) and $12,000+ (secondary); China, $2,200+ for primary-level students and $4,799 at the college level (2024).

What is the graduation rate for public high schools by country?

U.S., 87 percent; Finland, nearly 95 percent; Switzerland, 90 percent; Japan, exceeding 95 percent; China, 55–60 percent.

What are the differences in the education systems of the U.S. and developed countries with very low homicide rates?

U.S.: Values individualism, creativity, and critical thinking.

Finland: Prioritizes equity and a holistic approach, with a strong focus on student well-being.

Switzerland: Places greater emphasis on vocational education and training and personal skills at a young age, while the U.S. prioritizes academic excellence and standardized testing.

Japan: Emphasizes group learning, discipline, and conformity.

China: Focuses on academic rigor, rote memorization, and standardized testing, with an emphasis on a strong foundation in core subjects, while the U.S. system places more emphasis on critical thinking, creativity, and experiential learning.

School shootings: U.S., between 2001 and 2022, there were 1,376 school shootings; Brazil, 22 in 2023; Norway, 1; China, 1; Canada, between 1978 and 2018, there were 21 school shootings resulting in deaths.

10. Parenting: Aspects of a stable marriage relationship for children to grow up in.

What is the average percentage of new parents who were married prior to pregnancy, by country?
U.S.: 52%+ (2019); Finland: 43%; Switzerland: 70%–80%; Japan: 74% (2024); China: 69%.

What percentage of parents were still married for twenty years or longer?
U.S.: 50%; Finland: 40% (over 30 years); Switzerland: 30% (in 30 years); Japan: 23%+; China: no exact information found.

What are the statistics regarding domestic violence involving firearms in these countries?
U.S.: 1,300 deaths and 2 million injuries per year; Finland: 28 (2021); Switzerland: 41 (2015–2022); Japan: nearly zero, or a very small number; China: data not available.

11. How is social media different in developed countries with low homicide rates versus the U.S.?

Germany: Young people use it less than those in the U.S. and primarily to maintain existing relationships, while young people in the U.S. use social media for personal content creation and self-promotion.

England: Young people in the U.K. focus more on connection, conversation, and news, while U.S. teens are more likely to use social media platforms for self-expression and validation.

Russia: Teens in both countries use social media a lot, which can have both positive and negative effects. Russia relies largely on its own social media platforms rather than X (formerly Twitter), TikTok, or Instagram, which are widely used in the U.S.

South Korea: South Korean teens are more likely to use social media to maintain friendships and for entertainment, while teens in the U.S. are often more interested in building large networks of contacts. Social media appears to have a more positive effect on teens' mental health in South Korea, with a greater likelihood of negative effects on teens in the U.S.

Australia: Teens there use social media even more than teens in the U.S. and frequently use multiple platforms. The government is considering limiting or banning social media for teens under 16.

Beyond the original outline, here is additional information:

How have other countries that allow gun ownership, but have no constitutional provision like the U.S. Second Amendment, reduced gun violence through laws, cultural changes, or special requirements for firearm ownership?

Here are some examples; Australia, Japan, and the United Kingdom, and what they did to reduce gun ownership and, as a result, reduce the number of homicides in their countries.

Australia: Following the Port Arthur massacre (1996), the country's government enacted a law called the National Firearms

Agreement. This law restricted firearm ownership, prohibited civilian ownership of semi-automatic and automatic firearms, and established a national gun registry. It also introduced mental and physical health requirements, along with strict storage requirements, as part of its regulatory framework.

Japan: The law governing civilian ownership of firearms is the Firearm and Sword Possession and Control Law, passed in the 1950s. Handguns are not allowed except in very limited circumstances. Requirements include licensing, mandatory training, passing a safety test, gun registration, strict storage requirements, and mental and physical health evaluations. To purchase a firearm, one must be at least 20 years old. Gun use is primarily restricted to hunting and target practice.

United Kingdom: The Firearms Act of 1968 restricts ownership of handguns and requires a certificate from the police to purchase or possess a firearm or ammunition. The police assess an applicant's suitability by reviewing character, criminal history, and mental stability. This law has significantly reduced gun-related homicides and violent firearm use.

Findings and summation of material heretofore covered, and recommendations
One: The following aspects of the findings stand out most clearly:

    A. America has far more firearms in the civilian population than any other nation.
    B. America is one of very few nations that has a constitutional Second Amendment right for civilians to own and bear many types of firearms, including semi-automatic and automatic weapons, and even multiple firearms.
    C. Homicide rates in countries that ban or severely limit the right to own and possess firearms are very small compared to America's per capita rate.
    D. America's incarcerated population is the largest in the world, and its recidivism rate is high.

E. The number of children killed or traumatized by school shootings in America is much higher than in other developed nations.

F. Domestic violence involving firearms is significantly higher in America than in other wealthy countries.

G. Countries that allow gun ownership but do not have a Second Amendment–type provision in their constitutions have been able to pass laws regulating, restricting, and prohibiting who can purchase firearms, what purchasers must do to obtain them, and which types of firearms may be owned. These laws often ban certain firearms, such as handguns, semi-automatic, and automatic weapons. As a result, those countries have reduced the number of homicides, mass shootings, and incidents of domestic violence.

Summation: It is evident that the United States has a very permissive legal framework that has, for centuries, allowed for massive civilian ownership of firearms. This has resulted in over a million citizens being killed and several million being injured by gunfire, something no other developed, civilized country has allowed to occur within its borders. Why do we allow this? It does not appear to be beneficial in any way; rather, it is destructive and entirely unnecessary.

Recommendation: The United States of America must come to its senses in order to protect its citizens by addressing the Second Amendment to the Constitution. Doing so would allow laws, similar to those enacted in other nations, to be passed that restrict, regulate, and, when appropriate, ban firearms. Such changes would help modify our violent culture, making it substantially less violent and far safer for everyone.

CHAPTER TWENTY-FOUR

Contemplating adding more to his segment, Yoshi nevertheless kept Clyde's admonishment to be succinct in the back of his mind, so he prepared to forward his work to his companions in the Octogenarians Opines Zoom room.

KO: Your research sure discloses many imperative facts and data. Congratulations, Yoshi!

PM: Your segment is very informative. By the way, did you put up an eight-story edifice in Irvine not far from the beach? I was down there recently, and a friend told me he thought it was one of your developments.

ET: Good afternoon, gentlemen! Your segment reveals just how different—and, in many ways, far behind—other developed countries we are insofar as our culture is concerned. I was aware of how our education system ranks, but I was not aware of all the laws Australia, Japan, and the U.K. have passed regarding gun ownership. Thanks a lot for your revelatory segment.

Rx: I haven't seen so many percentages and data since I was in pharma school. Your segment is almost mind-boggling, YoYo.

YY: Thanks, everyone, for your comments. Yes, Mark, my company did construct an eight-story office building in Irvine that can be seen from Interstate 5.

SW: Good afternoon, everybody. Yoshi, I really am impressed by how well you constructed your information, arguments, and recommendations. Four stars to you!

KO: Isn't it amazing and unfortunate that we in America possess more firearms than the next five countries with large gun ownership combined?

YY: Yes, Roberto, those figures are astonishing. However, even with our 393 million guns, there are several countries, mostly in South America and the Caribbean, that have higher homicide rates.

ET: There's so much bad data in your segment, Yoshi, and one item that bothered me a lot is our country's education rankings worldwide. You pointed out our mathematics ranking. Some of our rankings are a bit better, such as reading, but considering how much we spend per student on education, we're not doing well.

YY: One thing to consider, Emily, regarding U.S. rankings in education is that our country has more immigrants coming in who don't speak English and, obviously, do not do well if they are not tested in their native language.

Rx: Hey, YoYo, you presented lots of numbers and statements without attributing them to any source. How are we supposed to give you any credibility without some verification?

PM: Clyde, you didn't provide any sources for your information either.

YY: Clyde, you may have missed my reference to Google searches as a source. Perhaps I should have been clearer about attributing almost all of my information to that platform. Due to my limited ability to read books and articles anymore, I had to rely on Google on my mobile phone.

Rx: PM, I'm a pharmacist. I know the information I included in my segment regarding drugs.

SW: We could debate all of this into the evening; however, I'm sure Emily and Clyde will want to have dinner soon.

KO: I agree, Shahzad. Perhaps we should talk about the future with your segment, which is of paramount importance. I believe you can come through as well as you and the other civil engineers did in New Orleans after Katrina.

ET: I share your sentiments, Roberto. However, before we leave Yoshi, I would like to know if you have any firsthand knowledge of any of the countries you refer to in your segment regarding their gun culture.

YY: Thanks for your inquiry, Emily. Yes, like most of you, I've been to several countries that I mentioned, such as Mexico, Canada, Scotland, England, France, China, the Philippines, and, of course, Japan several times. One thing that seems common to all of these countries is that I never felt threatened and don't remember seeing police officers or military personnel in uniform.

SW: That's been my experience too, as I have traveled internationally.

Rx: Okay, so you've answered the question. I could list a large number of countries, but it's time to concentrate on the future, as KO suggested.

PM: You have a way with words, Clyde. It's been my observation too, Yoshi, that law enforcement officers and the military aren't as visible in other countries as they are in ours. Shahzad, you have my trust as well.

ET: Those observations reveal an astonishing difference between our culture and those nations. I won't pursue this further so that Clyde can have his supper. Best wishes, Shahzad!

YY: Yes, Emily, the United States stands out in several ways compared with other nations, and our guns and crime are definitely part of that difference. I look forward to reading and learning from your segment, Shahzad.

SW: I hope I won't disappoint any of you and can make a worthy impact and contribution to our cause. Thanks, everyone, for your best wishes. I'll see you soon, I hope. Good night.

SEGMENT WRITTEN BY SHAHZAD IRAVANI

According to a Google search, "Since 1968, more than 1.5 million people have died from gun-related incidents in the United States. This number exceeds the total number of Americans killed in all U.S. wars." This number does include suicides. In Germany, during the same period, approximately 3,900 homicides took place. The suicide number is much greater. The U.S. population is around 335 million, and Germany's is 83 million. Which country looks safer to live in: the country that started the world wars or the country that was the winner of those wars?

According to Roberto's segment, guns started out in Asia and were spread worldwide by European countries. The English and Spanish brought firearms to our shores in the 1600s. Many natives, also called "Indians," were killed with those guns.

Then, when a country named the United States of America was established, a Constitution and then a "Bill of Rights," with ten amendments, were created. The Second Amendment was passed by Congress, allowing for the ownership and bearing of firearms by militia members. This has been a subject of debate.

Over the years of America's history, gun ownership became generally accepted, and court decisions did not restrict ownership to just militias. Then Americans really started killing each other with their firearms during the Civil War.

Following that war and decades into the future, guns became a bigger part of crime, as told in Mark's segment. Law enforcement had to acquire new tools and techniques to keep order. With the abolition of alcohol in the Eighteenth Amendment, the country experienced crime like that pursued by Al Capone's gang in the Saint Valentine's Day Massacre in 1929, in which seven men were killed with submachine guns.

New types of firearms were being developed and manufactured in the U.S. that could fire more rapidly, such as submachine guns that were more dangerous than present-day AR-15s.

Then we began experiencing mass shootings, like the one in Dallas and then the one in Virginia that Emily referred to in her segment. A mass shooting occurs when four or more people are killed or wounded, excluding the shooter.

Then came massive illegal drug dealing, which Clyde referred to in his segment, bringing even more homicides among gangs dealing in illegal drugs in large inner cities as a business.

At the end of the twentieth century, school shootings began to occur, like the one at Columbine High School, where two students killed 13 students and one teacher and wounded 28 with a semi-automatic handgun and two types of shotguns.

Organizations, as referred to by Roberto and Mark, went to courts and legislatures to try to interpret or create laws involving the Second Amendment to ameliorate and reduce gun violence in America.

Following that war and decades into the future, guns became a bigger part of crime, as told in Mark's segment. Law enforcement had to acquire new tools and techniques to keep order. With the abolition of alcohol in the Eighteenth Amendment, the country experienced crime like that pursued by Al Capone's gang in the Saint Valentine's Day Massacre in 1929, in which seven men were killed with submachine guns.

New types of firearms were being developed and manufactured in the U.S. that could fire more rapidly, such as submachine guns that were more dangerous than present-day AR-15s.

Then we began experiencing mass shootings, like the one in Dallas and then the one in Virginia that Emily referred to in her segment. A mass shooting occurs when four or more people are killed or wounded, excluding the shooter.

Then came massive illegal drug dealing, which Clyde referred to in his segment, which brought even more homicides among gangs dealing in illegal drugs in large inner cities as a business.

At the end of the twentieth century, school shootings began to occur, like the one at Columbine High School, where two students killed 13 students and one teacher and wounded 28 with a semi-automatic handgun and two types of shotguns.

Organizations, as referred to by Roberto and Mark, went to courts and legislatures to try to interpret or create laws involving the Second Amendment to ameliorate and reduce gun violence in America.

The NRA was created in 1871 to promote better marksmanship; however, in 1977 it became political, promoting gun rights and arguing against any gun restriction laws.

Groups such as the Brady United Against Gun Violence organization, which has a mission to challenge easy ownership of guns, was originally named the National Council to Control Handguns in 1974 and was renamed in the early 1990s. Other groups have been created, such as the Giffords gun control group and Everytown for Gun Safety.

It is all about the Second Amendment, so here is some in-depth information that my cohorts and I heretofore have not dealt with about it:

Produced by History Cooperative, the article is entitled "The Second Amendment: A Complete History of the Right to Bear Arms," written by Korie Beth Brown in 2024.

"One would think enacting legislation preventing such atrocities (Columbine High School, Pulse Nightclub in Orlando, Florida, or Sandy Hook Elementary School) would be an enormously smart career *move* for any smart politician. Yet senators and representatives routinely 'offer thoughts and prayers' for the victims, but nothing of substance has been done…"

"The reason? The United States is divided in its belief over the rights of individual citizens to own guns."

Both sides of the argument base their reasons on the wording of the Second Amendment itself.

"The history of the Second Amendment is long and twisted."

"In terms of wording, this statute is one of the most confusing. It's deceptively short, rather vague, and employs unusual grammar. Yet *over* the course of U.S. history, these 26 words have become some of the most controversial ever written."

If we look at all the circumstances, history, and needs of the government at the time, we may be able to see why the wording is somewhat confusing. Colonists had been living under the thumb of King George III of England, who had been infringing on their rights. Many needed guns to hunt for food, and the new government needed citizens to have guns for militias. So, several states included a right to own and bear arms in their constitutions, such as Virginia, North Carolina, and Pennsylvania, prior to the Second Amendment being adopted nationally and included in the Bill of Rights.

Moving a state's amendment into the Bill of Rights was mostly credited to James Madison (who at first, according to Google, had opposed that action).

The Bill of Rights was approved on December 15, 1791, by Congress to be part of the U.S. Constitution.

Many citizens owned guns they could use against the British forces who attacked the U.S. in 1812 and were eventually repelled.

With states beginning to create their own laws regarding guns, some of those laws were violated and challenged in state courts, and some cases reached the U.S. Supreme Court. The first court case involving Second Amendment rights occurred in Kentucky, named Bliss *v. the* Commonwealth in 1822. The ruling gave citizens of Kentucky the right to carry concealed weapons as part of their right to bear arms to defend themselves.

From that point on to the present, there have been many federal and state laws enacted and many court cases to determine the true interpretation of the Second Amendment, in response to circumstances such as the gunfight at the O.K. Corral involving Wyatt Earp, bootlegging involving criminals such as Al Capone and his gang, and much more: four presidents—Lincoln, Garfield, McKinley, and Kennedy—being assassinated with firearms; gang violence involving illegal drugs; mass shootings; domestic violence; school shootings; and more.

In 1868, with the passage of the Fourteenth Amendment to the Bill of Rights, it was made clear that states had to adhere to federal laws:

"No state shall make or enforce laws which shall abridge the privileges or immunities of the United States, nor shall any state deprive any person of liberty or property without due process of the law, nor deny to any person within its jurisdiction equal protection of the laws."

"The Fourteenth Amendment and the Second Amendment: This meant the Fourteenth Amendment was the first of its kind to explicitly guarantee rights to all people (of course, at that time, women did not have the right to vote)."

"The South bitterly resisted what it saw as an infringement on its rights to govern itself." The KKK and other types of organizations were created as part of that resistance.

The Supreme Court's decision in United States v. Cruikshank in 1876 was to protect citizens' constitutional rights by allowing states to create laws to do just that, including, of course, the right of citizens "to bear arms."

The Second Amendment in the twentieth century produced restrictions on owning and bearing arms, such as the National Firearms Act of 1934, which set regulations on certain firearms, including a tax on the manufacture and sale of some weapons such as machine guns, short-barreled rifles, shotguns, and silencers.

In 1968, the Gun Control Act was passed. "This piece of legislation repealed the Federal Firearms Act and provided provisions for the importation of guns and gun ownership requirements."

Changes in Interpreting the Second Amendment

District of Columbia v. Heller (2008), in which Justice Anthony Scalia wrote the majority opinion. He separated the two clauses and addressed only the second one. He interpreted the word "people" to mean "individual," making the right to gun ownership an individual right rather than a collective right for the purpose of maintaining a militia.

The Debate over Gun Rights:

"Do guns kill people, or do people bearing arms kill people? This is the crux of the current gun control debate.

Instead of owning a gun for self-defense or protecting the country from invading forces, a 2013 Rasmussen Reports poll indicated that 65 percent of Americans believe the purpose of the Second Amendment is to protect themselves from tyranny.

"Guns in American Culture"

To Americans raised on the idea of the Wild West, guns have always had a strange allure; changes in civilization have only further enhanced the conflation of "freedom" with "gun ownership."

"Not All Amendments Are Forever"

The Eighteenth Amendment was ratified in 1919, and it prohibited the manufacture, distribution, and sale of intoxicating liquor. The Twenty-first Amendment repealed the Eighteenth Amendment and allowed alcoholic beverages to be produced, transported, and sold in the United States. The amendment was ratified in 1933.

This concludes the information and views within the article entitled *"The Second Amendment: Complete History of the Right to Bear Arms"* that I wish to include in my segment. However, there are many more valuable details and information in it.

Two mass shootings took place in New Zealand in 2019 at the Christchurch Mosque. Fifty-one people were killed and 89 injured. The prime minister at the time was Jacinda Ardern. Within approximately three weeks, the national legislative body and the prime minister passed the New Zealand Arms Amendment Act, which banned semi-automatic weapons, reduced ammunition in magazines, included a large buyback operation, and generally imposed requirements for anyone wishing to purchase a gun in the country.

As a result of passing that new law, as of this moment, there has been a significant reduction in the ownership of semi-automatic weapons.

Have there been any mass shootings with semi-automatic firearms? Google: "No, there have not been any mass shootings in New Zealand with semi-automatic firearms since 2019."

In the same year, 2019, in the U.S., 211 people lost their lives due to mass shootings, and 1,643 people were injured due to mass shootings, according to sources on Google. Since 2019, over 2,300 people have been killed in mass shootings in the U.S.

Congress did try to pass two laws called the Enhanced Background Checks Act. One included background checks for firearms sold between private parties, and the second expanded the amount of time the FBI has to conduct background checks. Both bills passed the House of Representatives but failed to pass in the Senate.

Many have wanted the Second Amendment to be repealed. The following is from an article entitled *"Why a Repeal of the Second Amendment Would Not Be Enough to Stop Gun Violence"*:

"Laws alone do not stop violence, but voters and lawmakers must make common-sense legislative and constitutional changes that will save lives. As Thomas Jefferson wrote to Thomas Paine, the author of Common Sense, 'Go on then in doing with your pen what in other times was done with the law.'"

One suggestion for amending the Second Amendment comes from *"The Five Extra Words That Can Fix the Second Amendment"* by John Paul Stevens, a former Supreme Court justice.

Those five words are: when serving in the *militia.*

So, he is saying people should be able to keep and bear arms when serving in the militia. Does the full amendment, written in two clauses in a complex form, with the additional five words, make an understandable, reasonable, and grammatically correct thought?

"A well-regulated militia, being necessary to the security of a free state, the right of the people to keep and bear arms, when serving in the militia, shall not be infringed."

In present-day America, we do not even need a militia. We have several branches of the military; there is an Army National Guard in every state except Hawaii; states have police forces; almost all states have sheriff's departments within their counties; and, of course, any town or city of any—

CHAPTER TWENTY-FIVE

It took Shahzad several days to proofread and edit his segment until he felt somewhat comfortable submitting it to his fellow octogenarians in the Zoom room. At precisely 4:00 p.m. Central Time, he was in the room.

SW: Hi, Emily, it's good to see you again.

ET: Good evening, Shahzad. You must be a bit exhausted after all the research you did to create your fabulous and very inspiring segment.

SW: I'm not very exhausted, Emily; my old age has slowed me down a couple of measures.

PM: I completely understand what you are saying, Shahzad. However, your segment is remarkable in the extent of your research and especially your suggestions. Wow!

ET: This elderly lady also comprehends and shares your comments about being an octogenarian. I also agree with Mark about your segment covering so many aspects of the gun issue in our country. I'm grateful for our coming together to try to do something wonderful for our country! Hallelujah!

KO: Hi, everyone! Sorry I'm a bit late arriving. I had to pick up my grandson from a camp he was attending in the hills. Congratulations, Shahzad, on a very comprehensive presentation!

Rx: Your suggestion for the country to create an amendment is a little too sketchy. Have you tried to use AI?

YY: I really admire what you have done with your segment, Shahzad. However, perhaps we can all do some research to enhance your brilliant suggestion. I use the Copilot in Microsoft to correct my misspellings and punctuation errors, Clyde.

PM: Maybe our history professor can be our expert for what you are looking for as a workable solution to get an amendment passed without political interference. What about it, Roberto?

Rx: PM, you're willing to put all your trust in KO instead of checking out AI. That seems inadequate to me.

SW: We know what the Constitution states, yet I was hoping there is a magical way to circumvent the Article Five requirements.

KO: Shahzad, you've done your research, but unfortunately, except by an act of God, that is all we have to work with. I would also like to circumvent all the partisan wrangling in the legislature, too. Clyde can check with AI to see what astonishing suggestions it has to offer.

YY: Japan was able to implement significantly better gun laws, but it doesn't have a Second Amendment to deal with. It's the same situation for the UK: no right to own and bear firearms.

SW: So, Roberto, what do you suggest we do to get something passed that will significantly reduce the gun violence culture in the U.S.?

ET: I sure hope whatever we come up with as a suggestion for an amendment to the Second Amendment has a better chance of passing than the ERA of the 1970s.

PM: Emily, my memory is a bit fuzzy about that. Will you offer up the history and what the ERA was about? Sorry. Thanks.

ET: Sure, Mark. The ERA stands for the Equal Rights Amendment, which was intended to ensure constitutional equal rights for genders, not just males.

Rx: This is getting to be a distraction! Females already had the right to vote since way back when.

ET: Clyde, temper your cynicism. The ERA wasn't about voting; it covered other rights women didn't fully have then, such as employment, education, property rights, and even divorce. Men were being paid more for the same work women did, and that is still happening!

YY: Japan was able to implement significantly better gun laws, but it doesn't have a Second Amendment to deal with. It's the same situation for the UK: no right to own and bear firearms.

SW: So, Roberto, what do you suggest we do to get something passed that will significantly reduce the gun violence culture in the U.S.?

ET: I sure hope whatever we come up with as a suggestion for an amendment to the Second Amendment has a better chance of passing than the ERA of the 1970s.

PM: Emily, my memory is a bit fuzzy about that. Will you offer up the history and what the ERA was about? Sorry. Thanks.

ET: Sure, Mark. The ERA stands for the Equal Rights Amendment, which was intended to ensure constitutional equal rights for genders, not just males.

Rx: This is getting to be a distraction! Females already had the right to vote since way back when.

ET: Clyde, temper your cynicism. The ERA wasn't about voting; it covered other rights women didn't fully have then, such as employment, education, property rights, and even divorce. Men were being paid more for the same work women did, and that is still happening!

KO: That's a very good summation of the ERA, insofar as what I remember of it. Yes, it would be a great loss if our solution ended up like the ERA did. It seems we all agree that it's imperative that we try to do something about the unsustainable violent gun culture we have in our country. I think we all agree on that.

SW: Obviously, I do, Roberto. Do you suggest we just try to use the only written means we have available to us?

PM: Yes, Roberto, I'm with you one hundred percent. Let's give it our best shot!

YY: Since we can't circumvent the constitutional way of ratifying an amendment, we must give it a try as allowed.

ET: Yes, Roberto, let's see what we can come up with as a suggestion for wording for an impactful amendment.

Rx: Are you trying to take charge of our class, KO? Why don't we each try to write an amendment that would be sufficient for what we think is needed and get back to the room in a week or so?

KO: That's an interesting idea. I can participate in that challenge. How about the rest of you?

SW: I've already tried, of course.

YY: Good idea, Clyde. Okay.

ET: I might as well go along with you gentlemen and do it, too.

PM: As a former commander, I say, "Let's take it on!"

KO: Best wishes, everyone. If possible, we'll see what we can come together with within a week from now.

Rx: Don't cheat!

Exactly seven days later:

ET: Good afternoon, everyone.

PM: Hi, Emily. How did you do?

YY: I'm eager to see what you geniuses created.

SW: I ditto that, Yoshi.

KO: There are probably lots of A+ amendment suggestions. We can incorporate various thoughts from all of us into one workable, practical solution.

Rx: Don't get ahead of yourself, KO. I'll put my masterpiece out there right now: "According to Article Five of the Constitution and the Bill of Rights, amendments can be added to or amended in the Constitution. We, the people of the United States, hereby amend the Second Amendment to read as follows: The right to own and bear firearms can be restricted by Congress or state legislatures to provide for the safety and protection of their citizens."

ET: I like the safety and protection reasons, Clyde.

PM: "The Second Amendment to the U.S. Constitution is hereby repealed by this amendment. Laws providing rights to purchase and own firearms, and laws providing regulation and control over firearms ownership, shall be the authority of the U.S. Congress and state legislatures."

SW: Clyde should like your succinctness. I like your clarity. Here's my contribution:

"We, the citizens of the United States, hereby repeal the Second Amendment in the Bill of Rights of the United States Constitution."

YY: That is very clear compared to the Second Amendment, Shahzad. I guess I should attempt to present my offering, unless Emily wishes to go now.

ET: It is my thinking that it was men who created firearms, mostly men who used them in wars, who use firearms in domestic violence, street gangs, mass shootings, and crimes in this country. So, this female should just allow the male gender to resolve this issue solely. I pass. I believe in your commitment and competence.

KO: You have been such an integral part of our discussion and resolution. I think your idea on changing the gun ownership issue is vital to our summation.

Rx: I finally must agree with Roberto on this, Emily. We need your input as a female and a counselor.

ET: Sorry, gentlemen!

YY: "This Amendment is to provide safety for citizens and regulations for firearms ownership, manufacturing, and usage. The Second Amendment is repealed with this Amendment. All laws for regulations, requirements, and limitations shall be the responsibility of federal and state legislatures."

PM: Excellent, Yoshi. Now it's the professor's turn.

Rx: Make it succinct and precise. I need to have my dinner.

KO: "This (number) Amendment hereby amends the Second Amendment to state: The right of the people (citizens) to keep and bear arms shall be regulated and restricted by the U.S. Congress and state legislatures. The regulations, not limited to those listed, shall require sufficient criminal and mental health background checks; a permit to purchase any firearm; a gun owner license; registration of the firearm; and sufficient training on the proper use of the firearm to be purchased. Manufacturers shall be limited as to the types and models of firearms and ammunition they can manufacture, may be held liable for improper uses of firearms, and must install fingertip or other identification devices so that only the registered owner of the firearm can use it. All owners of firearms must acquire a license and register their firearms every five years with an updated background check. Firearms sold in private transactions must be recorded, and the new owner must be licensed. Governmental agencies must offer buyback programs."

PM: Whew! What a massive, comprehensive, and clearly written amendment.

SW: I was thinking, prior to reading your amendment proposal, Roberto, that we could incorporate various words, phrases, and ideas into a combined group amendment, but after reading your offering, maybe we don't need to endeavor to do that.

YY: My thinking leads me to suggest that we put all of our proposals for an amendment out there for all to read, see, and then come up with the best, most impactful amendment the country can use for our mission.

Rx: KO, you're back to being loquacious again. Your proposal is too long for the Constitution.

KO: Perhaps you're right, Clyde. I just wanted to get as many of the points covered.

ET: Thank you all for your compassion, dedication, and perseverance in doing something vitally important for our country. God bless all of you!

SW: Let's put all of our proposed amendments and segments out there and let others come up with the most successful one, as Yoshi said.

PM: I'll vote with Yoshi and Shahzad.

KO: Me too! Let's get the widest coverage we can—TV, radio, social media, podcasts, books, and certainly get it out there for Gen X, Y, and Zers.

Rx: Okay, I'm now going to have my dinner. SW, you didn't address the post–Second Amendment era in the U.S.

ET: I sincerely pray that our efforts provoke a metamorphosis in our gun culture, with more safety, trust, and freedom. What should we opine next? Good night, my valuable friends.

YY: Sayonara!

SW: Clyde, I thought I did by talking about Japan, Australia, and the UK with their significant gun control laws. Khodaa hafez, everyone.

KO: Yes, Shahzad, we got an idea of what things will be like with the repeal of the Second Amendment. Adiós, amigos, for now!

PM: Let's opine on DEI next month.

SHAHZAD IRAVANI
POST SECOND AMENDMENT ERA

Following the ratification of an amendment to the U.S. Constitution by thirty-eight states, or if the Supreme Court reads the Second Amendment correctly as intended by the original framers, some states will still have gun rights laws and/or some states will try to pass such laws. Gun rights lobbying associations will continue to support all means that allow people to buy, own, and carry guns. Congress and the states can then pass gun control laws without being as concerned about the Second Amendment.

If there is a president who supports more gun safety laws, the legislation passed by Congress will become law.

Some gun owners will protest, claiming that the government is coming after their guns and that they will fight back.

Buyback funds can be made available to pay for guns turned in to local police departments. It should be stipulated by the president that no guns are to be confiscated under the repeal law.

Gun manufacturers can be more regulated and be held liable in cases where their guns are used in homicides, etc.

Requirement for all new gun sales: safety locks and fingerprinting identity devices.

All guns sold as used at gun shows or privately must have a gun lock or other safety feature installed so that only the owner can fire the weapon.

Ammunition types and magazine sizes can be limited and defined under state or federal law.

Manufacturers of any component parts used in ghost guns can be sued and held liable and, if necessary, be considered criminally responsible.

The ATF and other federal and state agencies enforcing gun laws will be strengthened.

Culturally, we could try raising children completely differently, such as through James Kilgore's radical suggestions in his book Pedagogic Logic, or by adopting methods used by other countries to raise and educate children.

Without a Second Amendment, America will become more like other developed nations, with far less crime, fewer homicides, fewer mass shootings, less domestic violence, and a society that is safer, more protected, and more civilized.

ABOUT THE AUTHOR

When I was about thirteen years old, I went hiking with my older brother, Johnny, and a neighbor boy, Skipper. At one point, Skipper got ahead of Johnny and me. Johnny pulled out a small pellet pistol, aimed it at Skipper, and fired. Skipper dodged behind a boulder and yelled, "Stop it!" Watching that incident impacted me in a fearful way.

Following President John F. Kennedy's assassination while I was in college, and then Dr. Martin Luther King Jr.'s assassination, along with Robert F. Kennedy's assassination, and later President Reagan's assassination attempt, the Columbine mass shooting, the Sandy Hook mass shooting, the enormous number of homicides in Texas, and the daily violence that continues on and on, including the school shooting in Uvalde, I am now speaking MY MIND THROUGHT THE SIX FICTIONAL CHARACTERS IN THIS BOOK. in this book.

www.ingramcontent.com/pod-product-compliance
Lightning Source LLC
Chambersburg PA
CBHW060526160726
47991CB00001B/203